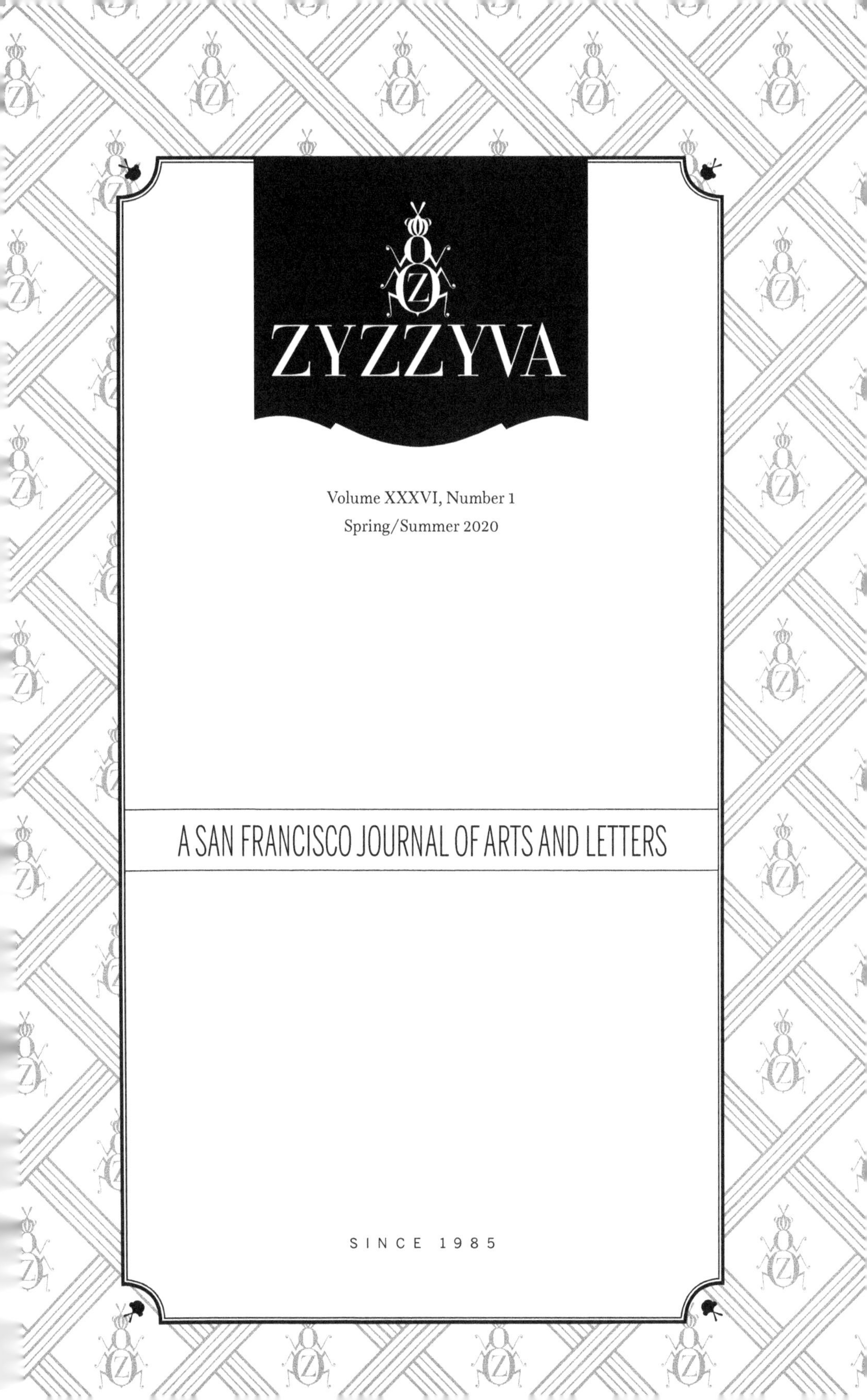


ZYZZYVA

Volume XXXVI, Number 1

Spring/Summer 2020

A SAN FRANCISCO JOURNAL OF ARTS AND LETTERS

SINCE 1985

# ZYZZYVA

**EDITOR**
Laura Cogan

**MANAGING EDITOR**
Oscar Villalon

**EDITORIAL ASSISTANT**
Zack Ravas

**SALES & MARKETING**
Laura Howard

**CONTRIBUTING EDITORS**
Andrew Altschul, Sam Barry,
Robin Ekiss, John Freeman, Paul Madonna,
Ismail Muhammad, David L. Ulin

**COPY EDITOR**
Regan McMahon

**INTERNS**
Alicia Long, Lindsey Pannor, Alecsander Zapata

**BOARD OF DIRECTORS**
Warren Lazarow, *President*
Laura Cogan
Patrick Corman
Jane Gillette
Regis McKenna
Barbara Meacham
Jonathan Schmidt

**ORIGINAL DESIGN**
Three Steps Ahead

**TYPE DESIGN**
Text font created specially for
ZYZZYVA by Matthew Butterick

**PRODUCTION**
Josh Korwin

**PRINTER**
Versa Press, Inc.

**DISTRIBUTION**
Publishers Group West

**SUBSCRIPTION SERVICES**
EBSCO

**ARCHIVES**
Bancroft Library, UC Berkeley

**CONTACT**
57 Post St., #604, San Francisco, CA 94104
**E** contact@zyzzyva.org
**W** www.zyzzyva.org

**SUBSCRIPTION**
$42/four issues; $70/eight issues
Student rate: $30/four issues

ZYZZYVA (ISSN 8756-5633) is published in April, August, and December by
ZYZZYVA, Inc., a nonprofit, tax-exempt corporation. © 2020 ZYZZYVA, Inc.

OUR PAPER STOCK is selected on the basis of its reduced
environmental impact. Text printed on Glatfelter Natures
Antique (30% post-consumer waste). Cover printed on
Kallima Coated Cover C2S. Both papers are FSC certified.

# CONTENTS

## VISUAL ART

Anne Siems, 137–144

## FRONT & BACK COVERS

Anne Siems, *Bite*, 2018, acrylic on panel, 48 × 48 inches, courtesy: the artist

Anne Siems, *Hear Me*, 2019, acrylic on panel, 24 × 24 inches, courtesy: the artist

## FORTHCOMING

No. 119 publishes in August, 2020.

# Zyzzyva.

*(ZIZ-zi-va) n.* A San Francisco
literary journal; any of various
tropical American weevils of the
genus *Zyzzyva.* The last word in
the Oxford English Dictionary.

# RARE BIRD

## CELEBRATING 10 YEARS OF ACCLAIMED STORYTELLING

EST. 2010

*"Wherever Good Books Are Sold"*

## JOSEPH DI PRISCO

*The Good Family Fitzgerald*

**APRIL 2020**

**ABIGAIL TARTTELIN**

*Dead Girls*

FIRST US EDITION

**EMILY STRELOW**

*The Wild Birds*

NOW IN PAPERBACK

**CHIP JACOBS**

*Arroyo*

LOS ANGELES TIMES BESTSELLERS

**SEAN PENN**

*Bob Honey Sings Jimmy Crack Corn*

rarebirdbooks.com

Stanford | Continuing Studies

ONLINE CERTIFICATE PROGRAM IN NOVEL WRITING

Embrace your literary aspirations
•
Develop the tools to write your novel
•
Work closely with Stanford instructors
•
Participate anytime, anywhere, online

Apply for the Fall 2020
Online Certificate Program in Novel Writing

Accepting applications April 13 through June 5.

Learn more: continuingstudies.stanford.edu

# NO, IT'S NOT CRAB FLAVORED.

IT'S JUST A FINE, QUADRUPLE DISTILLED, ORGANIC VODKA MADE ALONG THE EMERALD COAST OF HUMBOLDT COUNTY, WHERE THE REDWOODS OVERLOOK THE FRESH WATERS OF THE PACIFIC.

## AND YEAH,

THE CRABS ARE PRETTY GOOD HERE TOO.

**HUMBOLDT DISTILLERY**

# LETTER FROM THE EDITOR

Dear Reader,

This year marks the centennial of women's suffrage, and while it remains a source of national shame and outrage that we came by this expansion of voting rights so disgracefully late, it will nevertheless be natural for many to take the anniversary as a moment to celebrate how far we've come. But the passage of time has (or should have) also shifted our perspective and broadened our lens, so that what now stands in stark relief as we survey the landscape is how much work we have yet to do.

Some of this work, as Lauren Markham discusses in her essay, regards protecting and expanding voting rights, which are far from secure for so many marginalized communities. It's clear this essential, foundational aspect of our shared project of democracy requires ceaseless vigilance.

Less obvious, but hardly less essential, is the need to clarify and improve how we think about gender. This means advocating for the rights of women, but also bringing greater scrutiny to bear on how we frame both masculinity and femininity, and on how we raise, discuss, portray, punish, and support men, and what assumptions we perpetuate about masculinity.

Regressive depictions of masculinity abound in popular culture lately. Several of 2019's most celebrated movies make remarkably regressive portraits of masculinity their central motif: isolated white men whose interior lives appear inscrutable even to themselves, untethered by intimacy of any kind, violent, resentful. How we tell ourselves the story of who we are often reveals more than we intend, and judging by the stories told in popular culture, this country is both desperate for an overdue reckoning regarding its toxic narratives of who and how men should be, and violently resisting that push for change.

When male is the default gender, the experiences of all of us who do not identify as male are blatantly marginalized. But such privileging of one idealized archetype of gender also, more subtly, pins men into a corner, allowing absurd expectations of masculinity (which benefit neither men nor women) to persist largely unexamined and uncritiqued. Increasingly, studies suggest that even men who successfully perform cultural expectations of masculinity (stoicism, bravado, athleticism) and adhere to such social norms pay a substantial internal price. And when their mental and emotional health is most at stake, men are less likely to ask for help than they might be in a culture that allowed such expressions of vulnerability from them. That this internal damage can all too often spill out and take its greatest toll on men's closest relationships should be no surprise.

The quest for equality requires constantly refocusing our vision to understand what we've left out, and to see what, despite our best intentions, we've been blind to before. Advancing workplace protections and pay equity for women is part of the equation. Demanding consequences for abuse of women is part of the equation. Recognizing that an insistence on a binary notion of gender is at best reductive and unrealistic, and at worst cruel, is part of the equation. And dismantling centuries of assumptions about what and how boys and men should be—this is surely part of the equation, too.

Amid our larger cultural, political morass, how heartening to read the stories, essays, and poems gathered here, many of which approach issues around the social construction of gender—its damaging clichés, its diminishing reductiveness, its outrageous injustices—with nuance and tenderness, and yes, with anger, but always with humanity and from unexpected angles. This is, I think, exactly what we hope for in reading literature: to broaden our perspective, sharpen our vision, and deepen our empathy and sense of connection with other humans, living different lives from our own.

Which brings me to another anniversary of note: 2020 is our thirty-fifth anniversary in print—a milestone we're delighted to celebrate with everyone who has shared in this endeavor with us, from contributors who've trusted us with their work, and donors who've trusted us with their gifts, to each and every reader who has trusted us with their time. Thank you.

Here's to the progress we've made, and to doing better, and more, in the next thirty-five—and one hundred—years.

L.

# BEHOLD US TWO BOYS SITTING TOGETHER

DAVE MADDEN

Two years ago, I stood in a hotel bar looking for my best friend. I went down a dead-end hallway, then retraced my steps, and around a corner I saw BJ and his wife sitting far away at a back table. They'd come that night from a Capitals game, and I'd come from my conference hotel, and around our hugs and hellos I felt this air of cunning, as though we'd pulled off some scheme getting to be back in D.C. together. But it was chance, lucky timing. Beage and Wendy in matching fan jerseys. Young men in tuxedo shirtsleeves and women in heels filled the Hotel Monaco—the dregs of some wedding's afterparty. Beage and I ordered beers and Wendy ordered a G&T, and after the second round she was ready to call it a night. "Have fun," she told us, and told BJ he was driving home in the morning, hangover or no. Old friends, we rummaged through our shared pasts, filling in the gaps of the other's forgetting. What was the name again of that old roommate you had? Was that our senior year science project, or was senior year when we made everyone stay up all night to study sleep deprivation? The table's votive candle haunted BJ's face the rare times I'd remind myself to look at it. We'd never been eye-contacters. Then a moment landed between us like a duck shot out of the air. He told me, over the club music's scrunching, that he knew he'd been an embarrassment to me.     

"I know you were always embarrassed of me," maybe he said.

What was he talking about, embarrassed?

Beage waved me off. "I'm just glad we're past it and still friends."

Then he asked me how my job was going, and the moment lifted. We left before last call. My mom once told me she envied my friendship with BJ. "You went to grade school together and you're still friends," she said. "After all these years. Don't you feel lucky?"

I do. BJ and I are a triumph, probably.

That conversation took place two years ago, but Beage and I have never talked about it. I'm about to tell you about a friendship that's lasted thirty years and perhaps the first thing to learn is that there are certain subjects we don't talk about directly. Are we embarrassed? I think about that word and I'm back in high school, where I had a hobby of taking spent spiral notebooks and filling each page with a question I thought hard to make provocative: *What was/is the best thing about your childhood? If you were a bagel, what flavor would you be?* I'd pass the notebook around to my friends for answers. In one such notebook I kept a little poem I'd written one afternoon in math class:

"To Bayote"

I want to live
I want to sing
I want to laugh
I want to sting.

*Bay-yote* is a phonetic way to say, in German, "BJ," who was the first person I then handed the notebook over to. How can I explain? In those years, I paired one plaid vest over another plaid hoodie, wrapped both in a black cardigan rotted with holes, and finished the look with jeans I cut the hems off of so that the fringe would hang over the Converse

18  high-tops I wore every day. The stranger I looked, the better, because I felt stranger than my peers, and how could those happy people make fun of what I'd already made a joke of? I practiced this difference like a faith; it was how I spared myself from facing my frightful queerness. When BJ also wore Converse, I didn't see us as friends with things in common, I saw myself repeated, like a stutter.

*If you were in Heaven, who would you visit first?* was one of the last questions in the book.

BJ answered, "My best friend (if he's already dead)."

My answer? "The man in charge in order to find a way back."

After college, I tried to write Serious Fiction of the kind I was reading about in New York magazines, and for my MFA applications I wrote a short story about us—or rather, about a guy named Charlie whose boyhood friend Kyle drives up from Virginia one weekend to help him paint his Pittsburgh apartment. I wrote it just weeks after BJ had come to do the same thing. In the story, after the friends attend a party at the gallery where Charlie works, moods turn sour and the story ends in blood imagery, red paint smeared over both friends' faces. But the telling passage comes about midway through: "Growing up without a brother, Kyle naturally filled the role. I knew him better than anyone. Kyle's predictability bothered me for years and drove me away from home to find friends unlike him."

Yes, I showed him the story. Of course I showed him. Imagine your best friend writing this about you. What else could BJ think but that I was embarrassed of him? I've got thirty years of memories of being a bad friend that I could knit into a hairshirt to wear until the day I die—but only metaphorically. The only way I can wear my shame is to write this. *Exhibit number one is what the seraphs envied.* Or my mother, at least. Behold us two boys sitting together: Herndon, Virginia, 1988.

✳   ✳   ✳

I walked into my fourth-grade classroom and saw that all the desks had moved into a wide U that butted mine right up next to the desk of Brian, a boy I'd had second grade with but not third. Brian, I'd heard, went by BJ now. He had an elfin chin and high soft cheekbones, and despite what I much later came to learn was a Nordic background, his complexion was olive dark. One afternoon I heard him hum under his breath a song I was surprised to recognize.

"Is that Barry Manilow?" I asked.

"You like Barry Manilow?"

On weekends, my sister and I liked to put Mom's *Barry Manilow Live* record on 45 and stand on the ottoman to shimmy like Pentecostals to his commercial medley. *Giveyourface! Somethingtosmileabout! With Striiiiideeex.*

"My mom does," I said.

This was the first thing I came to know about BJ, who didn't live in my housing development. The sun-faced boys from my development who were good at kickball and commonly made other students laugh, boys like Todd Barnes and Jason Akana, didn't talk about Barry Manilow or even know who he was. When our teacher, Mrs. Warrenton—*Prudence* Warrenton, a gnat of a woman who glared at us through spectacles as wide as tea saucers whenever we talked out of turn—announced we were hosting a Mother's Day Tea, BJ hatched a plan: reenact our Manilow discovery with our moms sitting across from us, as though we weren't aware of the connection.

I loved the idea of telling our moms a lie.

He seemed to intuit that the fastest way to become friends was to get our mothers talking.

It worked. The next year, BJ and I sat together at the Hutchison Elementary Talent Show reciting the sketch he wrote: a TV commercial for the Ollie North Travel Agency. I didn't get any of the jokes, and we both failed to project our voices enough to be heard, we were told later, but we looked funny in the same striped shirt our moms bought at Hecht's: my stripes aqua, BJ's red. Hair the same shade of brown. Same scrawny frame. We could both take our right hand and wrap it around the back of our necks to bring it up under the chin and touch our right ear. We did this often, rarely by request, gangly deadman hanged by our own chokeholds. Once puberty raced through us, we started standing back-to-back—making sure not to touch butts—and asking friends in the vicinity who was taller. It was never an easy call for them to make. We were the same. We always looked the same.

But I felt different, for reasons it'd take many years to understand. I woke from dreams of butt-fucking Todd Barnes in my basement living room. "That's a gay dream," I wrote in my diary and tried my best not to have another. I knew that Todd Barnes was having no such dreams about me, and I suspected there was something behind this dream that could tell me why I was unpopular with my classmates. BJ, though, accepted me as I was. We saw in the other's body, in our need to get all hyper for attention, a shared social fate. By sixth grade the new thing among us nerdier kids was to say words backward, and mornings in Math Club, BJ waved to me and said, "Ih," and I'd "Ih" him in return.

In band, I chose the clarinet and he chose the trombone and we learned how to make music. Behold us two boys sitting together, hip to hip on a piano bench in the Cliffords' house in Reflection Lake on any snow day in the 1990s. Here we'd pretend we were Lennon and McCartney. Or Dolenz and Nesmith. BJ had all the fakebooks, and we skipped the songs about love for all the more knowing songs about shattering illusions. *Pleasant Valley Sunday. Fool on the Hill.* After he got a guitar and four-track recorder for Christmas, we moved to the floor of his walkout basement family room, surrounded by guitars. The snow would be piling up outside, we could see through the screened-in porch out back. His sister glued to her TV upstairs. Once, we tried a cover of "Nowhere Man," but I kept slipping my vocals up to the tenor, ruining us to unison. BJ rewound the tape: "Do you want to sing harmony?" We started again. Now I was flat. He took up his Gretsch and told me what buttons to press on the four-track so he could lay down the solo. He held it at the ready, earphones clamped on his head. The mic was next to his little Peavey amp. I looked into his eyes and waited for his nod. He nodded. I pressed the record button. Our voices, tinny, seeped out into the room through his headphones and I breathed very shallow so as not to make extraneous noise. I sat there and listened to BJ play the solo, brassy and languid, and he nailed it in the first take. He picked the last harmonic, let it sing out and decay, then nodded at me. I stopped the tape.

Where is it now?

✤   ✤   ✤

I have pages and pages of such memories. And yet, as "To Bayote" shows, underneath it lay this simmering rage. In high school, I auditioned to be the drum major of our marching band—the *Pride of Herndon* Marching Band—because participation in marching band was required for anyone wanting to play in the upper-level wind ensemble, and I wanted to play Rimsky-Korsakov and Mussorgsky instead of endless Sousa. I hated marching band's militarism and how it ruined music through all that strident brass. I hated being a faceless uniform stomping around a football field with a clarinet in my mouth. The drum major got to stand on the podium and tell everyone when to start playing; I had a strong enough sense of tempo to get the job my junior year, along with a senior named Dominique who, I learned, was of Caribbean descent and stood in her white pleather marching boots a foot shorter than me. We'd never once spoken, but now we had to march arm-in-arm, looking together like the top of a lesbian wedding cake. The next year, Dominique graduated and auditions were held for her replacement, and one guess who my fellow drum major was.

Imagine the competition judges beholding us two boys conducting together: precisely the same build and hair, the same gangly arms whomping through the air to lead the band through an accelerando. In my heart, I knew I was the senior drum major, with a year of experience on BJ, and I sported about the practice field with an air of relaxed entitlement. One afternoon in practice, I was facing a line of trumpets, who at this part in the show were turned away from BJ on the sideline. I conducted crisply and wide, holding steady at my own tempo, and the drill instructor shouted over his P.A. to stop, stop, *stop*. The trumpets were half a beat out of sync. I furrowed my eyes at them until it became clear who he was yelling at. Me. I was the problem. "You need to keep your eyes on BJ!" he yelled. "I don't want you looking anywhere but right at him!"

I learned to look at him, to *follow* him, and we won every Best Drum Major trophy (save one, he recently reminded me). As mirrors of each other, we were a success, and for a boy hung up on what shared Converse might reveal, this felt like dying. Here's how bad it got: from age eleven I'd begun writing letters to the University of Virginia asking for their course catalogue and admissions materials, dreaming of someday having what it took to get admitted. Then, senior year, I was.

And BJ was.

And he accepted the offer.

And I saw my future stretch before me like a flat, snowy expanse. I would not get to reinvent myself in college. I would not get the new life I'd been dreaming of. I would be in High School Part II, BJ's continued twin. *Kyle's predictability bothered me for years and drove me away from home to find friends unlike him.* Pittsburgh was a city where I knew no one, and this should have been when we drifted apart, right, BJ? Why didn't we drift apart? You and I both have plenty of friends we lost contact with in college. When I try to pinpoint what it was about you, or about me, that kept us together, I lose the pin. I can't imagine not being your friend. I try it, and it's like imagining not having arms, or a foot. A worrisome question at the heart of every relationship: where do they end and I begin? For so long, you always ended over there. Like: right over there in a very clear place I could point at and walk someone over to. But over thirty years, I feel that things have shifted, and there's a worrisome question left for me now: what is it that still lies between us?

And which of us put it there?

✡ ✡ ✡

In 2001, fresh out of college, we left our jobs and drove BJ's Audi around the country, visiting friends and other towns named Herndon. Side-by-side we were there with each other as we saw so much for the first time. Rice paddies. Center pivots. Red-winged blackbirds. Redwood trees. The Grand Canyon. The Pacific Ocean. The Texas Highway Patrol K-9 Unit. Idaho. To find our Herndons, we used road atlases, AAA guides, Mapquest printouts—ending up one hot afternoon in a dusty gulley west of Abilene, parked by an abandoned trailer in spitting distance from some train tracks. *Herndon, Texas?* We took our photographs. This was before cell phones, as people my age like to say, but that's not exactly true. Beage had his girlfriend's cell phone kept in the center console for emergencies, or for evenings at discount motels when he'd step outside before bed to check in with her. I had nobody but my mom to send postcards home to, so as I lay in bed reading comics, he'd pace the parking lot trying to hold his relationship together. It crumbled on that trip, breaking up fully in Oregon, the farthest from

24    home we'd drive that month. Hours after some sudden brake trouble set BJ back a grand, he went outside with the cell phone while my friends and I played a board game; and an hour later he came back in tears, dumped. I felt angry that she had ruined our trip, but also unpained by this news: Beage had been, since middle school, a serial dater, never alone for six months. Soon after we got back home, he'd find another woman I'd see as another rival for his attentions.

After Oregon, we hurried home to save money and face. One night out West, the highway empty but for our headlights, we broke a long stretch of silence to talk about the lives we were driving back to. I'd quit my job in online content back in Pittsburgh to come on this trip. Beage was on unpaid leave with the county and didn't want to go back. It was clear, I said, that his passions lay in music—he'd brought two guitars and a banjo on the trip, just in case we felt like recording something. Music had been his major in college. Why wasn't he trying to make it his job?

"A job is a job," he said. "It's what I do to pay my bills. Music is my life. If I made my life my job, if I relied on it for money, I think I'd come to hate my life."

It was pitch black out, the dashboard's glow lit our faces orange. I was struck by the force of his voice, the volume of it in our little car. I'd rarely heard him talk that way. And then I was struck with a feeling, a new one. Behold us two boys sitting together, as different as heads and tails.

❀   ❀   ❀

A friend in need is a friend indeed, they say, and I never understood it. Just because you help a needy friend doesn't mean he'll be a good friend back; witness any number of people you help move who then flake on *your* moving day. Then I saw I'd been reading it wrong: not A Friend Who Is in Need of Something, but rather A Friend Who Is

There in Your Time of Need, and suddenly it all came together. And then I felt ashamed. Had I ever been a friend in need?

When I at last allowed myself to say "Okay" to being gay, I knew I had to tell somebody and I knew precisely the somebody I would tell. I wrote Beage a letter and then deleted the file. Then I wrote another one I revised five or six times until one day I said "Enough" and printed it out and dropped it, terrified, into a street mailbox—my fear so great, like a taser jolt coursing through me, that I had to fight to let go of the envelope. I was afraid he would reject me. I told myself he had every right to—all those years of lying to him!—and I told myself I was strong enough to handle the loss of my friend.

A couple of weeks later, he called me on the phone. "I don't know what to say," he said, "but I just want to be here for you."

It worked. The first way he was there for me was by saying yes, still, to the two of us. The second way was rhetorically—for the rest of the year I was able to tell everyone, "I came out this spring," or, if they knew him, "I came out to BJ this spring." Never "I'm gay." "I'm gay" was much too difficult. BJ was there as the indirect object of my verb. There are days when I consider my life in the closet to be non-canonical, a prequel someone else wrote on spec. I sort of wasn't born until my twenty-sixth year, is what I'm saying, and if that's true then BJ was the first person to see me alive. My doula.

My partner and I have an understanding about new couples we spend time with: we're not really friends with them until we're safe in knowing they're unshockable. If I open up and confess that I think abortions should be free at any neighborhood pharmacy, or that I had another sex dream about Jim Belushi, a friend accepts these as part of my character. Anyone else is an acquaintance I now need to be not-myself around. In this, there's a tribal quality to friends, a cliquish tendency, which everyone who's written on friendship is keen to explore. C. S.

26 Lewis, a writer BJ loves but I've never been able to get excited about, writes about "the attitude of the majority towards all circles of close Friends."

> Every name they give such a circle is more or less derogatory. It is at best a "set"; lucky if not a *coterie*, a "gang," a "little senate," or a "mutual admiration society." ... Of course this is the voice of Envy. But Envy always brings the truest charge, or the charge nearest to the truth, that she can think up; it hurts more.

What hurts more is to read this and not find in our friendship a recognizable portrait. The objective of BJ was never to retreat into a haven of mutual regard, the objective was to fill the time I'd otherwise spend alone. Weekends. Snow days. The parts of Thanksgiving break that weren't Thanksgiving dinner. BJ was there, available. And sure, while we've racked up whole loads of inside jokes, something in his spirit or character must have attracted me and held me as long as it has. Something more than familiarity. With what adjectives would I finish the sentence "BJ is ______"? BJ is understanding. BJ is accepting. I knew in my heart he'd never reject me, and this is why I told him before I told my family.

But these are mirror traits. BJ understands me. BJ accepts me. In youth, the mirror of him reflected my surface and I turned away in fear that this was the sum of me, but in adulthood, that mirror reflects so much of my history that I worry every time I write about Beage I'm Narcissus at the pond.

A person is not a mirror.

That something that's between us? What if I let it be a peephole?

✳   ✳   ✳

Let's be Beage. Age forty. White. Brown hair. Six feet tall, maybe two-hundred pounds. Married twelve years to the girl we got set up with after college, who teaches history to middle school kids. Let's live in a townhome in a suburb of Washington, population 71,000, with our two sons, Oscar, nine, and Jack, four, and our dog, Melvin, and drive thirty minutes to work at an engineering firm, where we and the team we lead help rezone properties for developers to build what they're dreaming of. Let's drink beers at our work lunches, wear sideburns that border on muttonchops, and buy a leather iPhone case that looks like an old prayer book. Let's believe in God, but skip church. After the kids are in bed, let's record songs on our iPad in our basement, where our kids keep all their toys and we do the same, our guitars and amps and accordion and pedal organ and our bottles of Scotch tucked away in closets and cabinets. Let's mow our own lawn. Let's have a car payment. Let's have a mortgage and a habit of railing against home ownership, which we call a crock. Let's have, overall, a softness that makes us attractive in a spatial sense, makes it easy for people to want to get close to us. Let our talents glean to music, and let's develop those talents to where we can pick up any instrument handed to us and play "I'm a Believer" or "In My Life" well enough for everyone in the room to sing along. But mostly, let's play those songs alone, in our basement, our friend since fourth grade living 2,800 miles away, where his guitar case sits behind his bedroom door, coated in dust.

✿    ✿    ✿

In adulthood, Beage has grown more of a body than I have. He has bulk in his chest and shoulders, his ass, that may be more beer-won than gym-won, but it's there. Mass on a man's body is something I've always been both drawn to and cowed by. We, as I've said, rarely touched growing up, but these days I hold his body in my arms when I come back home and see him again. He feels in my embrace both

28 sturdy and soft. A ripe avocado. BJ has a posture when he walks that looks marionettey in how it plucks up his shoulders. It's not a stoop so much as a vampiric prowl set at ease by the languidness of his shuffle, the whole body galumphing up and down like a Max Fleischer cartoon. He chews gum while he drives, plucking a hardshelled piece from one of those short plastic canisters that fit snugly in his SUV's cup holder, using an empty one against his driver's-side door to spit the gum out into. It's disgusting and charming. What I like about BJ's body is that it's a part of him that is no part of me, unshared, unhistoric. As friends we weren't curious or daring about our bodies growing up, never talked in sleepovers about hard-ons, never circle-jerked or used each other as practice bodies before girls became available, and while I've retroactively fantasized about having such a friend growing up, I wouldn't have wanted this in BJ, knowing instinctively how it would have spoiled that something that's between us I'm trying to capture here. In college, drunk one night in our friend's pool, we all shucked our suits and swam naked for a stretch, and while I didn't want to stare, I took stock in where Beage and I stood and found myself—dickwise, I mean—coming up short. I didn't feel envy or inadequacy, and I didn't necessarily feel proud of him. In between these poles stood something else. Call it fraternity. Or *fraternité*, if it helps. In me, a man who confuses sex with affection, it involves a stunning discovery: I don't want to fuck this man I like. In the aftermath of that explosion, a dust settles, and in its place lies comfort and intimacy.

Once, I and a friend of ours blindfolded BJ and drove him somewhere deep in Fairfax County, the end of some generic cul-de-sac inside a nest of twisting cul-de-sacs. We set him in a car, made him wait a few minutes for us to drive off, and then let him find his way back to a bar in Herndon. If he made it back in one hour, we'd buy his beers that night; if not, he was buying. The friend and I drove back in my car, excited

about the contest, feeling pretty good about the confusing place we
dropped him. I parked in a lot across from the bar, and as we walked
toward the entrance, guess who was standing there waiting for us.



His whole thing is zoning, land use. A master's in urban planning.
I go to him now with questions on density and development where I
once had questions about Debussy, Dvorak. On another work trip back
home, I'd been taken by conference-goers someplace unfamiliar and the
plan was for BJ to meet me there. When he showed up, I asked if he had
trouble finding the place. "No, we did all this," he said, gesturing at the
entire shopping center. The "we" was the engineering firm he worked
for. "I can't tell you how many hours I spent in meetings talking about
that parking lot." We sat across from each other, us two boys, slower and
mellowed, the mirror of each other patina'd by time and our distance.
Later that visit, I met him and the family to watch Oscar play soccer, a
gorgeously perfect suburban thing I wanted for the gorgeously perfect
fall day. I arrived late and walked over to the far end of the field, where
I found BJ wearing an orange plaid shirt that looked vaguely familiar.

"Was that my shirt?" I asked and he nodded. I'd given it to him
back in college. It looked so warmly worn, so softened in the flannel.

It fit him perfectly, an old friend on an old friend.

My mother calls BJ my brother from another mother, and I'm
called the same by his mother.

Growing up, imagining a wife-and-kids narrative for myself, I
dreamed of having twin sons.

I am a Gemini. (BJ's a Cancer.)

There's a framed photo of us on my desk here, in matching tuxedos,
taken in the Shenandoah hills on the afternoon of his wedding day.

We look cute together; people mistake it for my wedding photo.

That day, I was BJ's Best Man.

My toast told the story of our road trip, bickering over career paths.

30

BJ started a new job recently, working for a law firm.

Once, at a previous job, he fell in love with a coworker, and he called me, sobbing, after her last day in the office.

That love never turned physical, and that amazed me, that self-control.

That understanding.

Beage was the first person I told about my years of cheating on my partner, confessing over the phone while I crashed on a former student's sofa for a week.

"I'm going to text you every day for the next week or so," he told me.

"You don't have to respond, but I want to check in and make sure you're okay."

I like to think I returned the favor when he called me in tears about his coworker, when I told him everything he was feeling was okay, that falling in love is okay, that being able to love more than one person is a good thing because it means you're full of love, not empty of it.

And then I said, as we were hanging up, "I love you."

And I had never said that to him before.

"I love you, too," he said.

Friends in need.

✻  ✻  ✻

San Francisco butts me up every day against more people than I've ever had to live among, and yet here I find myself friendless. I have colleagues, professional contacts, former students. There are couples my partner and I fail to make plans far enough in advance with, and so end up spending another weekend at home, in front of our TV set, behind separate laptops scrolling through digital media, where "friends" abound. If we were straight, we'd have made a child by now, or two or three, and let friends fall to their supporting roles, replaced by the stars of Family. But we're queers, freed from the trap of biology. For us queers, the project is to escape the biological family—the *heteronormative* family—and replace it with accepting friends, fuckbuds, lovers. Despite growing up in a supportive one, I'm suspicious of family, because I've learned the codes. *Family First. Focus on the Family.* Pro-family spaces have long been anti-queer spaces, and yet given the chance to spend just one snowy afternoon playing guitars with Beage in the Cliffords' family room, I'd run back in the closet, however that might work.

I mean the Cliffords of Herndon, Virginia. The Cliffords of my youth. I forget that those Cliffords no longer exist, BJ's parents long divorced and each remarried, his sister renamed by her husband. BJ's wife and kids are the Cliffords now. Their family room has toys all across it, plastic playsets, a low table painted with a winding racecourse. The mornings I visit and crash on the futon down there, I wake and swing my legs off the bed's edge and sit in my briefs for a minute. Groggy, hungover. From upstairs fall the screams of brothers failing to play fairly. Once again, I feel out of place. Misfit. A queer among a family. All of BJ's friends back home are other dads, and together they caravan their families on weekend trips to cities near amusement parks, they grill out in the backyards of the homes they own, they dogsit for each other. It's fair to say I envy him. BJ has the house, the backyard, the multiple bathrooms. He has the two sons I wanted. They're not twins, but close enough. I watch him be a dad with them, like I would a creature in the wild. He'll get stern to teach them manners—*say thank you, ask to be excused from the table*—and then scoop one up and toss him, cackling, on the sofa. He's attentive but not coddling. He's there in the way we want dads to be. Those two boys are so lucky.

BJ's achieved his narrative trajectory. He got what he wanted, and I'm proud of him for it. I got maybe half of what I wanted. I got the life in the city. I got the art career. The parts I didn't get I know that Beage

32 is always willing to share, as he always has, ever since the beginning, his house open to me every snow day. In Herndon, we got maybe two or three of them a year. The news came over the TV in the morning, and I'd call his house to verify what was already understood: I was coming over. There were songs to work out on the piano, games of Pit to play, and Careers. I bundled up in coat, scarf, and gloves and walked through the nicer half of Seasons Four, where the houses were three stories and made of brick, and down at the end of one cul-de-sac I stepped around a wide barrier and stood suddenly at the end of a cul-de-sac in Reflection Lake, the snow shimmering, like in the back of a wardrobe.

The Cliffords had the Swiss Miss packets with mini marshmallows. They had Intellivision and a fire going, usually, his mom home from her job as a school librarian. No matter what room we sat in I felt a part of that house, that family. Given the chance I may have chosen them. The Cliffords had Jeno's Pizza Rolls and a screened-in porch out back, under the deck. When we felt the need to get outside, to enjoy this cold weather that had given us the gift of a free day, BJ and I put on coat, scarf, and gloves and sat in the two hammock chairs that hung out there. It'd be 11:45 on a Tuesday. The sky was thick and opaque like raw wool, and the ground was a shag carpet, and the air around BJ's house was so completely still that we only had to whisper to be heard. Between the two of us sat nothing but the sound of snowflakes hitting the ground. That *tsst*. ❧

*Dave Madden is the author of the story collection* If You Need Me I'll Be Over There *(Indian University Press) and* The Authentic Animal: Inside the Odd and Obsessive World of Taxidermy *(St. Martin's). He is an associate professor in the MFA program at the University of San Francisco.*

# JUDITH SAYS // LET'S HEAR IT FOR THE GIRLS

## MEG HURTADO BLOOM

*thoughts on* kunst, *Giselle, & the Supreme Court of the United States*

What's harder to believe than Woman? Only the world.
Lucretia, Persephone, Debra, Giselle—all those girls who've been had.

Say their names; say "this happens," again and again.

About suffering the masters were wrong, too:
it leaves a mess. No damask dress

can staunch the wound, and a mother
can shove a lord, but only once harm's done.

Remember every penetrated breast, certain doom's
the only accepted testimony. Recall the queen of the dead,

brought down by a single seed.

We turn eyes to the sky but only because
we are tired. We are not confused.

Time we trashed our veils, filled the forest.
So many of us that we're deathless these days, and

damage takes chances, keeps that last dance
looping till dawn. We can do this. We have washed

34    so much blood from so many clothes.
We will name our daughters Judith.

We used to love him but we had to kill him,
new songs will say. We will light something,

stand in our jammies, ask Judith to steady our hands.

Sometimes she holds a clean sword and nobody's dripping head,
Sometimes her belly is wrapped in gold,

Sometimes she and her maid look like
they could be in a kitchen, slicing ham[1].

So many ways to paint women's work.

Yet whether she's feeling herself,
or kinda not sure she just did that—she's done.

---

1   *Caravaggio's Judith is among the most honest, despite the depiction being by a man. It is said that he was able to paint Holofernes's spurting blood because he had attended the public beheading of one Beatrice Cenci, a beautiful Roman teenager who murdered her abusive aristocratic father.*

# HEAVEN IS FULL OF GARBAGE DISPOSALS // PRAYER FOR LORENA BOBBITT

## MEG HURTADO BLOOM

It all began with cherry blossoms,
cake, a swimming pool.

It began again by refrigerator light, as so much does.
From bed to kitchen—longest walk.

The men will say you gotta build
a legal bridge from battery to righteousness, but why?

We all held the knife. We were grateful.
Witness after witness sang of bruise after bruise,

parading reasons she didn't need.
Sometimes you gotta kill a mood.

She cried and the country cried back.
She made sure the carving was clean.

In heaven, we won't call her crazy to save her.
In heaven, she'll cut loose again and again.

*Meg Hurtado Bloom's writing has appeared in* Split Lip, Lumen Magazine, *and other publications. Her poetry appeared in the Bay Area Issue (No. 117).*

# WORK NIGHT

## LYSLEY TENORIO

Maxima in the dark. Half-lit by a Virgin Mary night-light and the glow of a screen saver, a slow-motion sweep of stars and planets—Jupiter, Saturn, Earth. Dressed in denim cutoffs and a Mickey Mouse tee, she doesn't shiver, despite her wide-open bedroom window and the cold night beyond. She sits at the foot of her bed, cleaning her nails with the tip of a switchblade. *"May bakas ka bang nakikita so aking mukha?"* she sings. *"Masdan mo ang aking mata."* Like all her favorite Filipino love songs, this one is about heartbreak.

An alarm goes off. The digital clock glows red—10:10 P.M. She closes the switchblade.

She stands and stretches, takes quick jabs at the air—*one-two, one-two, one-two*—then flips on the desk lamp and sits, turns on the ball-shaped webcam atop her monitor. A tap to the space bar and the galaxy vanishes; now her face fills the screen. Using it as a mirror, she puts on maroon lipstick and dabs with a Kleenex, smiles wide to check her teeth. She undoes her ponytail and shakes out her hair, a long black wave, then turns her face side to side, searching for her best angle. She could easily pass for thirty but is somewhere in her fifties; her true age, she swears, is a mystery, even to herself. Her parents, long since dead, kept no birth certificate; the grandmother who took her in never bothered to learn her actual birthday.

Eyes closed and fingertips on the keyboard, she whispers to herself, so softly that a person standing next to her would have no hope of knowing what she says. She takes a deep and slow breath, opens her eyes, types and clicks until another browser window opens.

There is a man on the screen.

"My love," he says.

"No," she says. "In Tagalog."

"Sorry. Hello, *mahal*."

"That's better." She blows him a kiss.

"Oh, mahal, please don't tease. It's been a lousy few days."

She leans into the screen. "Ano ba? What happened, Henry?"

"Where to start." He removes his glasses, the stubbly flab of his cheeks moving up and down as he rubs his temples. He pours a shot of Jack Daniel's into a coffee mug and recounts his terrible week—more layoffs at the plant and all the guys blame him, his ex-wife trashed the Miami timeshare but won't pay for repairs, his Benz is still in the shop and the best rental he could get is a three-year old Camry, and just today an invitation to his high school reunion—"My freaking fortieth!" he says—arrived in the mail. "But the real downer"—he gulps the whiskey—"is the weather. End of spring and I'm still shoveling snow."

"*Snow, snow, snowy snowy snow,*" she sings in a made-up tune. She puts her elbows on the desk, rests her chin on clasped hands. "My whole life, I never see snow."

"Come to America. To North Dakota."

"One day. If God is good."

"God is always good." He pours another shot, doesn't drink. "Come closer. I want your face to fill my screen."

She leans into the webcam, so close she could kiss it. He says she is the most beautiful woman he has ever seen.

These past three weeks of talking online, he says, are the best he's

38 had in years. A twice-divorced balding white guy on the edge of sixty doesn't hope for much, but when he found her profile on Good Catholic Filipinas and saw that her favorite food was sweet-n-sour chicken, that her favorite singer was Shania Twain, and that her lifelong dream was *"to live in joy with a good man in God's country,"* he convinced himself to send her a message. "It's silly to reminisce," he says, "but life before you seems so long ago. I didn't realize how lonely I was."

"I was lonely too," she says.

"And I think that maybe, well, probably, that I might be"—he takes a deep breath, takes the shot—"falling in love with you."

She pulls away from the screen.

"I'm sorry," he says. "Too much, too soon?"

She shakes her head. "Not too soon, mahal. I think, maybe, that I am falling in love, too."

"With … me?"

She laughs. "Yes, with you. Tanga!"

*"Tanga?"*

"It means 'stupid.'"

He lets out a breath, slaps his chest twice. "My heart. It's racing."

"'Heart.' In Tagalog, *puso*."

"Puso." He writes the word down. "That means 'heart.' Got it."

"Soon, you'll speak Tagalog. Then you can visit me in the Philippines, di ba?"

"Or you visit me first. Maybe you can be my date to the reunion?" He sets the scene: he enters his high school gym to the tune of his old prom song, "We've Only Just Begun" by the Carpenters, and though he hasn't aged as well as his classmates, there's no question that he has the sexiest, most gorgeous woman in the room on his arm. The other women are jealous of her, the men envious of him, and the bullies from his freshman year just stand to the side, giving him the thumbs-up.

"And the whole night," he says, "you and I just dance."

He leans into his webcam. His whole head seems to inflate on Maxima's screen. "When can we meet?"

"Philippines to America," she sighs, "not so easy trip." The lines in Manila for passports and visas take hours, she says, sometimes days (that's just to apply), and never mind the near-zero chances of government approval. Their best hope for being together is to pray, to keep faith in God, and to wait. "And when I come to North Dakota," she says, "will you show me the snow?"

"Count on it."

"Okay. But one condition only: I don't shovel."

He laughs, which makes her laugh, harder and harder until she's hunched over, laughter becoming gasps for air. "Mahal," he says, "you okay?" She shakes her head, takes a breath and says it's nothing, then keels over again.

"It's definitely not nothing," he says. "What's wrong?"

She looks straight at the camera. "I'm hurt."

"Hurt? Hurt where?"

She clears her throat, takes a breath. "Don't worry, Henry. It's nothing, okay?"

"Stop saying that. Just tell me."

She looks at him for a moment, as though wondering if he can be trusted with something as private as pain. "If that's what you want, mahal"—she stands up—"then okay." She lifts her shirt slowly, adjusting the camera to make sure he sees, then turns in a slow circle to reveal a wound, a crusty gash that spans from the top of her hip to the middle of her abdomen. She explains: It happened in the typhoon two months before. A snap of bamboo, sharp as a spear, sliced across her body in the high-velocity winds. "I lost so much blood," she says. "But I'm thinking, okay lang, it's just a cut, bahala na. Pero now, I have an infection." Her own grandmother, she tells him, died from an infected cut, but God's good grace will keep her alive, she's sure of it.

She lowers her shirt and sits. "But every day it hurts."

"What can I do? How can I help?" He slumps in his chair. "I hate this. I *hate* being so far from you." Before she can speak, he says that maybe the day to meet should come sooner than later; what if this is God and the universe telling them that he should be the one to fly to her and, depending on the current round-trip airfare from Grand Forks to Manila, now is the time to come together? But Maxima says no and promises him that there's a better day ahead for them to meet, one when she is healthy and strong. For now, all she needs are his love, faith, and prayers. Nothing else.

"But there is one thing," she says.

"Tell me."

"Medicine. Ointments and creams with all the antibiotics. The best hospital in Manila has them. Pero"—she bites her lip, fighting tears—"walang pera."

"*Walang pera?*"

"No money." She shakes her head. "There's never money."

Henry puts his glasses back on. "Well, how much do you need?"

"Bahala na, mahal, it's okay. Please don't worry."

"How much. Tell me."

"I can't accept." She swivels her chair away from the screen. "I'm too ashamed."

"Just tell me. Please."

She takes a deep breath, nods. "Twenty-two thousand pesos."

"Pesos? How much is that?"

"Four hundred dollars." She turns back toward the camera. "USD."

Henry says nothing, just listens.

"Half the money for the doctor, the other half for the medicine," she says. "In the Philippines, if you have no insurance, medical care is very expensive, it's almost impossible, talaga. It's not like in the States." She dabs her eyes with her pinky and, with her other hand safely out of camera view, reaches for the switchblade next to her computer. She flicks it open and twirls it between her fingers, a thing she does when anxious or uncertain, when the inevitable is on the edge of finally happening.

On-screen, Henry is motionless, his face a blank. "Mahal," she says, "are you there?"

Finally, he moves. "I'm here," he says, "sorry. The screen froze for a sec. Where were we? What were you saying?"

"Money. For the medicine."

"And how much was it? Five hundred?"

"Five, yes," she says, nodding. "Five hundred. USD."

He looks toward the ceiling and blinks, like he's adding up figures in his head. "Let's make it six hundred, okay?"

"Six?" She shakes her head, says no, no, no, starts to weep. "It's too much, mahal, too much—"

"Sshhh," he says, a finger to his lips. "There's no price on love, *di ba*?"

She laughs. "*Di ba!* Yes, that's right." She wipes her eyes with a Kleenex, says it's almost one P.M. in the Philippines, time for her to go. She gives quick instructions when and how he can wire money to an online account, tells him she'll let him know when the payment goes through. "This will help me so much. Thank you mahal, thank you," she says. "And soon, one day, I promise, we will meet."

Henry nods. "Yes, mahal. And when we do, we'll sit in the countryside, put on some Shania, and then"—he leans into his camera, filling her screen again—"we're gonna fuck like bunnies." He winks and kisses the air, and the blade spins faster in Maxima's hand.

They say goodbye and Henry signs off, disappears from the screen. But Maxima is still there, and for a moment she watches herself, tilts her

42 head slightly, like her face is one she recognizes but doesn't quite know.

She turns off the webcam.

She lifts her shirt, carefully peels away the wound, a trick of rubber and glue, then jots down quick notes in a small spiral notebook. She picks up the switchblade and opens her closet, where on the inside of the door she's tacked up a human target, the kind found at a shooting range. She steps back, stands against the opposite wall.

She raises the blade, aims, and throws. She misses the heart, but not by much. ✀

*Lysley Tenorio is the author of the forthcoming novel* The Son of Good Fortune *(Ecco) and the story collection* Monstress *(Ecco), named a Book of the Year by the* San Francisco Chronicle. *"Work Night" is excerpted from* The Son of Good Fortune.

# ZAPRUDER FILM BLOOPER REEL

## TROY JOLLIMORE

*What like a bullet can undeceive?*

—Herman Melville


The shooter forgets to take the shot.
The president forgets to fall.
The pink sleeve of Jackie's suit gets caught
in the door. The man on the grassy knoll

neglects to reload. He misses the shot.
The man on the sixth floor neglects to reload.
He misses the shot. Jackie's sleeve gets caught.
The president gestures to her in code.

The crowd of bystanders, primed for a show,
forgets to be shocked. The president falls
so gorgeously they erupt into
spontaneous, heartfelt applause.

The lighting is wrong. Jackie misses her mark.
The president stumbles over his lines.
We lose the light. The image goes dark.
The rifle jams. The Director resigns

himself to another take. The man
pauses to reload on the grassy knoll.
*This country,* he says. *They can put a man
on the moon, but you can't make him drink.* The role

44

of the second shooter will now be played
by a stand-in whose name everyone forgot.
He hits his mark. His image fades.
The shooter forgets to make the shot.

The A.D. calls *Cut!* The Director calls *Action!*
Blood and flesh light up the screen.
The image for this week's Write Your Own Caption
Contest is frame number 313.

The camera jams. It's a beautiful shot.
He watches it pass from the grassy knoll.
Jackie nails her lines. The image is caught.
The Republic forgets, or does not, not to fall.

*Troy Jollimore's most recent poetry collection is* Syllabus of Errors *(Princeton University Press). His essay, "Shawn's Last Night," appeared in the Resistance Issue (No. 111).*

# CATHEDRALS OF HOPE

LAUREN MARKHAM

In 2004, when I was first old enough to cast a ballot in a presidential election, I lived in a small Vermont town, population 1,136. It was home to farmland, a cemetery, a snowmobile shop, a church, an elementary school, and a town hall that most days sat empty and unused. The leaky clapboard house my three roommates and I rented was shared with mice that ate through our cupboards and a badger who lodged in an unfinished back room. My roommate Margaret used to sunbathe on our lawn to the occasional honk of a passing car; we all enjoyed cigarettes on the porch, puffing our smoke into the world, watching it drift to someplace far away. To counteract the cigarettes, I liked to take long runs through the dairy fields, stealing some time alone up and down the dirt roads, through the undulating green and the snow. On Election Day, the start of Vermont's interminable gray November, I slipped my ID into my sports bra and took off running into the fields on a route that would deliver me right to the town hall where I could vote before returning home to change and head to class.

Inside the town hall, I was greeted by a volunteer dressed in flannel, who gave me a piece of surprisingly large paper and pointed me toward a row of curtained cubbies. The curtains were made of tattered red, white, and blue fabric draped over an old curtain rod, and in each cubby a pencil was tied to the table with a long piece of yarn. I made my choices

46 and folded up my ballot small enough—which took several creases—for it to fit into the slit of the padlocked wooden ballot box. It was all so analog and wonderful. I waved goodbye to my fellow voters and the volunteers, to whom I felt deeply connected in the moment, regardless, I felt, of who we were all voting for. As I left, one of the poll volunteers, an octogenarian with a wide smile and a slight hunch, handed me a handmade popcorn ball wrapped in cellophane. Voting even came with party favors. Democracy! I was entranced, I was hooked.

And then the results began to roll in.

I had voted for John Kerry. I didn't love Kerry but I hated George Bush and all his administration stood for: imperialism, racism, idiocy; a thirst for money and for war, all in the name of our supposed protection. (In this way, my first vote—something that had been hard-won by generations before me—was a lesson in settling.)

My friends and I had been so certain the presidential election would go our way. Our class had started college in the fall of 2001, just weeks before 9/11, and our sophomore year was marked by war. Our whole emergence into adulthood was mired in violence and senselessness and vendetta. We'd do something about these garbage politics dominating the airwaves because, goddamn it, we could vote. My friends Sam and Andy threw a voter registration party; they printed out registration forms from all fifty states and set up a table by a trashcan full of punch. Sam had become certified as a notary the previous week so he could notarize the forms and mail them the next day. We were going to vote and we were going to win.

When they called the election, we were devastated. *Four more years, of this?* (We had no way of knowing, even then in our despair, just how long the shadow of that result would stretch.) We lost. That's what democracy is—accepting the possibility that you'll be on the losing end of the tally pile. The next day, a group of us gathered to mourn and smoke cigarettes outside the dining hall. My friend Kevin read Ginsberg's *Howl* out loud, screaming into the darkening day. It felt poignant at the time, and then quickly and for many years after, I remembered it as a baroque absurdity. Now I look back at that moment with tenderness. *"Who fell on their knees in hopeless cathedrals praying for each other's salvation and light."* At least we felt it.

And we were looking for precedents, for guideposts, for elders to help us navigate from the misery we felt toward some brighter future. Our professors didn't much have what we were looking for, nor did our parents. I had a crush at the time on an older writer I'd met at a party who sometimes came into town offering motorcycle rides and compliments and tales of his adventures. After the election I logged onto a library computer and, helpless and hopeless, wrote him about the "sad sad times." "Don't worry about the sad sad times," he replied. "Or, more correctly, worry but don't despair. We have to fight harder and more fearlessly." I felt acknowledged and like I'd been given a mission.

Since that day in November, I've voted in a school cafeteria, in a school basement, in a church, in my own garage. Each time I marvel at the persistently analog nature of the vote and feel, however fleetingly, that I am stepping into some collective current, turbulent and unfinished and sacred. I recall that warbling enthusiasm in my chest when I first voted, like I had been handed a torch to carry forward.

Democracy is messy as hell and, in an increasingly antiseptic world where so many rites have been converted to transaction, I can find in its messiness something to celebrate.

As in: when my great grandmother arrived to this country from Greece in 1914, no voting for her. As in: my grandmothers were both born when women weren't allowed to vote, but one of them lived long enough to watch her granddaughters cast their ballots.

For many years, I've worked at a school for newly arrived immigrant

48 youth, many of whom arrived (though under far more dire circumstances) like my great grandmother did—alone, raw with hope and with the uncertainty of their futures, their first moments in the U.S. lived from within the inside of a detention cell. Even when they turn eighteen, the vast majority of my students won't be eligible to vote, and won't ever be able to vote unless (or until) our immigration laws change dramatically. (A hope horizon can recede so quickly.) The asylum process is being eviscerated, immigrants are being harassed and beaten and murdered in the streets and in their schools and in their homes, they are dying in detention and being forced to wait interminably for "their turn." Though they live here and work here and pay taxes, my students seem to have fewer protections every day. On the 100th anniversary of women's suffrage in the United Sates, democracy is, in so many ways, a myth, a sham. Yet another reason to fight harder and more fearlessly.

To secure the Vote for Women, suffragists lost jobs and partners, were shunned by family members and friends and excommunicated by their churches over the right to vote; they were arrested and laughed at and called heathens and beaten and slandered and force-fed in their prison cells. "The present agitation," Susan B. Anthony proclaimed, "rises from the demand of the soul of woman for the right to own and posses herself." A radical notion. Prison sentences were long and harsh for suffragists; their food was infested with worms; guards brutalized them while many Americans looked on in scorn. My ability to take a little jog to my polling place and cast my ballot required so many before me to fight without fear—or to fight *with* the fear that neglecting to do so would lead to things staying the same. How easy human beings can forget the people who came before us, and the debts we owe.

"It was we, the people," said Anthony, "not we, the white male citizens; nor yet we, the male citizens; but we, the whole people, who formed the Union. ... Men, their rights and nothing more; women, their rights and nothing less." A 1917 protest sign: "They say we are a democracy, help us win a world's war so that democracies may survive. The women of America tell you that America is not a democracy." How many people today, amid our voting restrictions and our gerrymandered districts and our electoral system and our impossible immigration exclusions, feel the same way?

Like all history sealed into our textbooks, the stories we tell about women's suffrage also deserve some revisiting. For while the passage of the Nineteenth Amendment was a victory for some, it was, as social victories so often are, won at the expense of others. It was a victory for white women, who betrayed their fellow black suffragists. This fact is often erased, and is sometimes cast as the slow, piecemeal nature of progress—first things first, then the next things after that.

"Throughout much of the first generation of the women's suffrage movement," writes Rosealyn Terborg-Penn in her book *African American Women in the Struggle for the Vote*, "Blacks attempted to demonstrate that disfranchised African Americans and disfranchised women shared the common plight of oppression. In doing so, they aimed to unite the two groups for a greater driver toward universal suffrage." But when unity became less politically advantageous, the dominant white women's suffrage activists threw the goal of universal suffrage out the window.

Once the Nineteenth Amendment was passed, black women suffragists appealed to members of the National Women's Suffragist Association (now the League of Women Voters) for support. "As many Black female suffragists suspected," wrote Terbord-Penn, "white women voters ignored their plight. Having earlier encouraged Black women to join the movement in order to bring Black male voters into the women's suffrage camp, white suffragists then abandoned" them.

If a myth is a story we write backward to explain—to justify—the present, then too often the history we teach in schools is the stuff

50  of myths—whitewashed, saccharine, clean narratives of righteous struggle tied up with a bow. Many of us were taught that the women's suffrage movement was led by Susan B. Anthony and Elizabeth Cady Stanton, and that it began at the 1848 convention of Seneca Falls. Yet few revolutions have such a clear genesis. In her book *The Myth of Seneca Falls*, historian Lisa Tetrault reveals that though the Seneca Falls Convention certainly happened, Stanton and Anthony fashioned the event into an origin story some twenty-five years after the fact in order to control the suffrage movement narrative. "The mythology Stanton and Anthony created has, in turn, sanctified them," writes Tetrault, "so that it can, at times, be uncomfortable to see them as complex political actors, driven by an ambition to lead and animated by the self-assured knowledge that they knew best."

How do we celebrate progress and honor our predecessors while also acknowledging that progress's casualties and its tactics of exclusion? It would be easier to do this is if we were better trained to do so early on—that is, if our schoolbook history was approached with some degree of complexity. You know who, if given the chance, understands the complexities of politics better than any of us? Teenagers, the students themselves. They are weathervanes of sincerity and hardwired for justice. What's fair, what's right, whom should we trust, whom should we believe? Ask a teenager, she'll tell you. But we rarely ask.

Just because someone is legally permitted to vote doesn't mean they will be able to. In 1870, the Fifteenth Amendment passed, making it illegal to bar people—defined as men—from voting based on "race, color, or previous condition of servitude." Still, many black men were barred from voting. In 1887, Native American men were eligible for citizenship so long as they disenrolled from their tribes; the Citizenship Act of 1924 granted voting rights to all Native Americans, but it wasn't until a 1948 court case that actual voting rights were secured, and even then, not in every state until 1962. In 1920, the Women's Suffrage Amendment was passed, but still, black women and other women of color were largely barred from voting. In 1943, Chinese Americans won the vote. Until then, the laws hadn't fully recognized them as citizens, which is to say, people.

Today, many Native Americans still cannot vote because some reservations do not use formal street addresses; thus, their voter registrations are rejected. Tribal ID cards aren't valid forms of identification according to the Voter ID laws in many states. Since 2010, fifteen states have used the specious specter of voter fraud to launch stricter voting laws, requiring a government-issued photo ID and so setting a bureaucratic hurdle that disproportionately affects low-income people and people of color. Meanwhile, the national Republican State Leadership has redrawn voting maps in places like Ohio to keep a stranglehold on power there for years to come. "As a result of the new map," writes Alora Thomas-Lundberg of the ACLU, "Republican candidates earned 51 percent of the statewide vote in 2012, but secured 75 percent of the state's congressional seats." Earlier this year, courts lifted a decades-long ban on Republicans' use of "ballot security measures," which is Republican-speak for voter intimidation.

It's so important to name that things have gotten better. But has anything really gotten all that much better? Despair edges in. These hopeless cathedrals, us down on our knees.

The 2016 election casts a terrible heap of shadows, one of them being that too many people have been tricked into believing they witnessed the beginning of a catastrophe, rather than a subsequent chapter of a catastrophe already underway. Because we teach such tidy history in our schools, all steady arcs and epiphanies and heroes and villains, this kind of thinking is an easy trap. But November 6, 2016, took a magnifying glass to what was already there and enlarged those injustices to Godzilla-size.

Everyone has a story about the morning after. Mine was we were set to host about thirty visitors at our school's annual open house (that we'd scheduled the open house the day after the election was, in retrospect, an act of hubris.) Who did I know who had slept? Who, that early morning, wasn't walking around as if on a faraway planet's sterile moon? I didn't want to talk to anyone. I bought myself a rare cup of coffee. (I'm a tea drinker, but, desperate times.) Outside the coffee shop an unwell woman shouted obscenities at no one in particular, and took her empty beer bottle and flung it against the curb, where it shattered.

Many of our students had predicted the election's outcome long before it came time to vote. So when they came to school they were angry, and bereft, but, unlike many of their teachers, not particularly shocked. Their concerns were pragmatic and urgent. Were they safe out on the streets, they worried, in their homes, in this country? Fair questions. No one was quite sure what to do with her rage or sadness. Students began painting their faces, making protest signs from scrap paper and recycled cardboard. They marched down Oakland's Telegraph Avenue, cheered on by shopkeepers and passersby.

"They're going to send the Salvadorans home," one student said to me.

"I told you so," said another. "I told you he would win."

When the election was called the night before, the California polls hadn't even closed yet. The pizza we'd ordered had just arrived.

A myth: our vote counts.

A myth: our vote doesn't matter.

"Did you expect us to turn back?" yelled suffragist Elsie Hill toward an approaching mob at a 1917 demonstration. "We never turn back … and we won't until democracy is won!"

Democracy is spoken of as this absolute entity, this inherent good. But like all human inventions, it is only as good as the people upholding it.

The vote: how can it be true that something is sacred, and sullied? How do we acknowledge the criminal, restrictive state of things while also holding on to the possibility that there is, somewhere in this vast dungeon, a little shard of light? What's hard is to continue to believe that the shard of light will ever become anything more than a shard of light.

"This is an extraordinary time full of vital, transformative movements that could not be foreseen," wrote Rebecca Solnit. "It is also a nightmarish time. Full engagement requires the ability to perceive both." Solnit also said that a vote isn't a Valentine, but a chess move. This serves as a reminder to me that the immense privilege of being able to vote in this powerful country means that I should wield it. But it would be nice to feel like a single vote could be both a chess move and a Valentine.

I felt as much in 2008. For me, the world was plumped with hope. I drove to Nevada to campaign for Obama, and, at the Reno headquarters, was instructed to drive an hour west, and then once there, I was dispatched another hour south into the flat, dry, painterly hinterlands of the southern state. My coworker Diana and I went door-to-door in the trailer park communities to speak with people about the upcoming election. One woman told us Obama spoke with a forked tongue. Another proclaimed that there was no option but Obama. Yet another expressed concern Obama would take her guns away, based on an article she'd read in a magazine. (The magazine, which she showed us, turned out to be a gun catalog.) One man we spoke to was a veteran who wanted a candidate with military experience. Another guy was on the fence; was Obama too young to run this country, too green? As we walked the dusty roads with our clipboards, dogs rushed from their porches and from under their trailers, howling, nipping at our heels, forcing us, from time to time, to run for it and pray. I was back in that hurtling current of history and of purpose. *You must fight harder, and more fearlessly.*

54 And since then? That rushing slipstream can be hard to come by. Some days, seeing all the ways our country, our world, rips its people to shreds and brings us to our knees, I catch myself feeling that perhaps it's best we all just burn so the Earth can have itself back without the human scourge.

The author Alexander Chee wrote on Twitter: "Your cynicism is only ever an in-kind donation to your opponent, posing as independence." And a few months later: "After a week of holiday conversations about the election, I just want to say cynicism poses as rebellion while supporting the status quo."

"A radical idea: vote your conscience in the next primary," read a recent op-ed in the Texas Observer.[1] We are so focused on who is electable that many who would vote Democratic are not voting according to what they want, but according to what they think other people will want. *I like this candidate, but I don't think he/she could win,* says my father, my godfather, so many people on the news and on the internet and at the dinner table. How can anyone stand a chance of winning if so many insist he or she or they can't win?

A myth: "Perhaps this country just wasn't ready for a black president." This is a thing certain people sometimes say; they generally say this when no people of color are around. *Perhaps we're not ready for a woman president. A radical. A socialist. A Latino. Someone so young. A woman of color.* This sets my skin on fire. It sets my skin on fire while trawling Twitter, at my extended family's dinner table, in an imagined conversation on the street. *They* won't vote for her. For him. This amorphous *they,* this *them.* Who are they? "We are *they!*" my brother and I insist to our dad one night at a bar. "I am *they!*"

This bloodless calculation isn't the chess move Solnit is talking

---

1 *https://www.texasobserver.org/a-radical-idea-vote-your-conscience-in-the-presidential-primary/*

about. And isn't it the opposite of fearlessness? Of course there's so much to fear. But if we act only in fear, don't we just end up with more to be afraid of?

"A better way to do this—the way a primary is supposed to work," the op-ed reads, "is for each voter to support the person they feel is the best candidate, under the theory that if enough people agree, they probably *are* the best candidate."

Did people struggle for my vote—did people get trampled and bloodied and arrested and force-fed and betrayed and left behind to struggle alone—so I could imagine what some hypothetical person far away might be imagining that some other hypothetical person wants in a candidate? Or did they struggle so I could vote my goddamn heart? I'll never know for sure, but I'll choose heart every time.

In 1920, a group of women marched toward the New York Metropolitan Opera to force President Woodrow Wilson's hand into calling a special session of Congress to discuss the Vote for Women. They were met by the police. Suffragist Doris Stevens recalled: "Clubs were raised and lowered and the women beaten back with such cruelty as none of us had ever witnessed before ... Women were knocked down and trampled under foot, some of them almost unconscious, others bleeding from the hands and face; arms were bruised and twisted." *The New York Times* headline the next day: "200 Maddened Women Attack Police With Banners and Fingernails." They were "maniacs who should be institutionalized," an op-ed read.

Why aren't more of us—why aren't I?— in the streets, putting our bodies more fully on the line for voting protections, for expanded voting rights, for a national holiday on Election Day, for a pathway to citizenship?

It's helpful to imagine what could come of it. One day, if we fight hard and fearlessly enough, more of the barriers to voting—all of our

56 own making—could come crashing down. Our cathedrals needn't be so hopeless. Because the young people I know—so long as we teach history rather than myth and don't infect them with our cynicism—will lead with the heart at the ballot box. And I'll be there, passing out the popcorn balls. ✄

*Lauren Markham is a fiction writer, essayist, and journalist, and is the author of* The Faraway Brothers: Two Young Migrants and the Making of an American Life *(Crown), which won the 2018 Ridenhour Book Prize, the Northern California Book Award, and a California Book Award Silver Prize.*

# MIMESIS

## DUJIE TAHAT

What if my lover raised me?
What if we two had a child
    so young,

I raised my lover, too?
I was born an older brother
    to a badly beloved,

and sometimes it's enough
that I remember her birth-
    day. By some

weight, I am a loving brother.
By nearly every measure,
    I am a cheap date.

My pocket's out. I spent it
all to feed my daughter.
    I mean son. No—

daughter. Which am I again?
At what ending do I begin? I
    think I'm here

for my hearing, Your Honor.
You need my sister's date
    of birth? Yes,

I was born with that name,
but, ma'am, America made me
    to respond

to anything odd, so forgive me
for a fraudulent citizenry. It's just
    the boy I was

is not the body I insist becomes
me, my sister, or my lover.
    He's not even

a boy anymore. Look at me.
Am I the mirror or the body
    in the mirror?

Can one divorce the thing
that happened to them?
    I rid myself

of a beloved once. Isn't that
plenty? The truth is I didn't
    want to be

a boy, a good American
brother, but I didn't know how
    else to dress.

*Dujie Tahat is the author of* Here I Am O My God, *selected by Fady Joudah for a Poetry Society of America Chapbook Fellowship, and* SALAT, *selected by Cornelius Eady as winner of the Tupelo Press Sunken Garden Chapbook Award. He lives in Washington.*

# SWAMP TYRANT

SANTIAGO JOSÉ SÁNCHEZ

The flies rained down on the van. They were jet black, peanut-size. Hundreds, no, thousands hovered over the wiry waves of grass unfurling at either side of the road like ambivalent helicopters over a sprawling yellow city. The flat distance was called the Everglades. A cold metal brace clamped around Santiago as he noticed Matthew's small white hand crawling over the middle seat toward his knee. Matthew was about to say something stupid, something that would land them in a pot of trouble with Jack, his stepfather. Matthew had warned Jack about the flies as they left Miami; he would know since his real father lived in Clearwater, which was somewhere outside of Naples, where they were headed in the little green van for a weekend camping trip. He wasn't the kind of man who took advice from a child. The skin around Matthew's nails was stripped back in pieces, the way their pencils looked after Jack used a knife to sharpen them. The closeness of this vulnerable detail stunned Santiago into stillness and attention. It was as if he had a paper bag over his head with a single tiny hole cut in the front, because he couldn't see anything anymore, not Jack, not Talia, nothing else of this van and family that was to him as strange as his own; it was all Matthew's fingers, a herd of red beasts nearing his thigh, and that one raw pinky arching to tap the pale inside of his leg, saying, *Watch me do something stupid.*

**60**  "How much was that car wash last week?" asked Matthew. He leaned into the middle seat, searching the rearview mirror with a smile on his face. Even his eyelashes fluttered, like a girl's, because this, too, pissed Jack off.

Jack, his hands at ten and two, choked the steering wheel. The leather squealed and the color drained from his dark fingers. He didn't turn around and wipe the smirk from Matthew's face with a solid slap. He stayed completely still, even as another fly crashed into the windshield with a hollow thud. Try as he did to hold himself still like him, Santiago jumped after each knock on the glass. It had to be another American thing, Santiago thought. Perhaps like Matthew, he, too, would one day back talk his mother. One day it wouldn't look bold or foolish but completely normal, even necessary. Another part, he thought, of becoming American. The gnawed pinky tapped his knee again.

"The car's gonna look pretty by the time we get there."

"Mateo," Talia said, moving her hand from her lap to the console between her and Jack. Santiago could only see the side of her face in the mirror. The flies stuck to the glass like boogers and mottled the light on her cheeks. She was still prettier than his mother.

"That boy is asking for a whooping," Jack said, and then to Matthew, "Smart mouth."

It was a thing Jack said often, which Santiago understood as a compliment since there wasn't an equivalent phrase in Spanish. Matthew had a voice and mouth he knew how to use. It was because he was born in America, because he had the green eyes, blond hair, and pale skin of his white father; because instead of going by Mateo, as his mother had named him, in school and at church, he was Matthew. Santiago couldn't believe his luck still, that out of everyone, Matthew had chosen him as his best friend. He thought, as he had a hundred times before, of the stories his brother told of their past in Colombia, even if he knew they were lies, like everything else that came out of his mouth. In his brother's stories, Santiago didn't cry when he was born and when it came time to speak he didn't. He was this close to being an autistic mongrel, his brother said one night, sectioning off an inch between his thumb and pointer finger, as if he had found the distance between two worlds. These lies rushed back to Santiago when he felt the balloon trapped inside of his throat, all hot air, which was often, since his own mouth was dumb.

"Can we turn the A/C on?" Matthew asked, changing strategies, a wildness in his eyes. The ripe, briny rot blowing in through the vents, mixing with the smell of French fries and sweat that the heat lifted from the beige upholstery, materialized again, summoned by Matthew. He held his nose at the bridge, pinched. He wasn't afraid of anyone, not even Jack. That's what he was trying to say. And Santiago loved it, that he could sit inside of a family that wasn't his own, feeling he understood them better than they did themselves.

"Oh wait, right, there's none. I forgot."

Jack lifted his hand from the steering wheel and the beige leather sagged in grooves shaped by his fingers. He held the knob of the fan, and stared back at Matthew through the mirror. *Look what you're making me do*, he said with his eyes, as he turned the fan off, punishing everyone. Beside him, Talia groaned, spread her legs, and leaned closer to her window. Matthew tore into his thumb again, the pink flesh sliding in and out of his mouth in maddening flashes. Santiago looked around the green van, at the dried leaves and McDonald's napkins strewn on the floor, at the windows that didn't go down. The clutter of clothes in the trunk, the indistinct crumbs in the cup holders, and the beige ceiling that sagged in the middle. It was these same intolerable things that he loved about them. Unlike his mother, who cleaned and cleaned, Talia didn't try to erase every sign of her family's life. She didn't need things to be perfect. She didn't need to cut clean from her life before this one. Santiago was six when they left Colombia. He had no memories of his own, and since his mother never spoke of the past, he only had his brother's stories to go off. In their kingdom, they'd had maids, the latest clothes and games shipped over from the USA, a second home with a sparkling pool in the lush mountains outside the city. His brother remembered a time when he was among the popular kids, where everyday after school, there were at least six boys crammed on the couch, stuffing their mouths with fries and racing cars on the television. His brother told him all of this in the apartment in Little Havana, where more often than not they found themselves alone, surrounded by the hum of the window fan and the yellow circle the bulb in the kitchen cast around them, like two princes waking up from a long sleep, realizing they were in exile. The lesson, at least as his brother meant it, was that their mother was a madwoman who had ruined their fortune. And so from the earliest of times, Santiago had known himself as the bastard son of a royal family and promised himself to be nothing like his mother, and especially, nothing like his brother.

Santiago turned to Matthew, who was examining the stud of blood gleaming between the torn white flaps below his thumbnail. He wanted Matthew to feel how he felt—lucky, grateful—even here, in the stench and heat, crossing this no man's land to a campsite in a place called Naples. He wished he could make Matthew as happy as he made him. His hand crept toward Matthew's thigh now. When the tips of his fingers graced the hem of Matthew's shorts, he held on, and nobody— not Matthew, not Jack, not Talia—noticed.

"You shouldn't have come," said Matthew, his knuckles white around the green garden hose, and the words, like a punch, left Santiago quiet as the air escaped him and slowly crept back in.

They had to wash the van, unload the chairs and cooler. Jack had delivered these instructions as if he were permitting them a place to sleep tonight, since nothing was a given with him when he felt the need to make his authority felt.

"I mean, sorry, you didn't have to come."

Matthew tugged on the green garden hose without looking back at the tangle caught around the water post.

"I know, I know. I begged you. I just couldn't have gone through this weekend alone."

Santiago didn't know what to say. Matthew always started with the sharpest version of his thoughts, then whittled them down until all the edges were lost. It was the bits splintered off in revision that Santiago kept and held on to, until he hurt inside. *Some things were too good to be true* and *Nothing ever did last,* he repeated his mother's skepticism to himself. He untangled the green garden hose, feeling small and useful, and stepped back as life surged through the tubing. From one moment to the next water ran through the hose. Matthew didn't question it. He simply dug his thumb into the narrow metal opening, forcing the water out in a jet. There was an emptiness in his eyes, like his mind was elsewhere. He crisscrossed the spray over the windshield, over the hood, down the chrome grill, over the license plate with the black frame that said "United States" and "ARMY" in yellow letters, cutting lines across the dense black carpet of flies. The water thundered over the metal.

"I would go anywhere you go," Santiago said, happy to be somewhere not home. He figured there was a reason to all this. Jack wasn't a tyrant. No one could be. Only love could run deep through a person. This was all a test. The way Jack treated them like men when they were just boys could be nothing less than a lesson on love. They had only to look closely, to rearrange the parts until they formed that picture. Jack was testing how far he could push the two of them to love each other—and how

64    perfect would it be if that were the case. Jack, tall, skeletal, impossible to miss in his uniform, could still be seen across the parking lot. A white wife-beater tucked into camo pants. A forest green explorer hat like a target hung over the back of his neck. He dressed no differently in Miami, and at first, Santiago had been struck by how whimsical, if not terrifically out of place he looked lurching the aisle of a grocery store or standing in line at the bank among men dressed in button-ups and khakis, polos and jeans. Now, he couldn't think of Jack without these clothes. They belonged on his body as the blue belonged to the sky. Jack craned his neck sharply then. He had eyes on the back of his head or shoulders, eyes everywhere. He swatted the air with his hand, which meant, *Get to work.*

Matthew scraped the last of the flies, the ones that didn't want to let go, with the edge of his hand. He snapped his wrist, casting the bodies off. The hose fell to the ground. Without a care for his leather sandals, he stomped through puddles to the back of the van. Santiago wanted to point Matthew's attention to the car ride, to every little thing he had said, and say, *Stop doing this to yourself.* He picked the hose up from the ground and turned the water off. He wondered where Matthew went when drawn inward, and why this wasn't a place they could be together. Santiago wound the hose around his arm the way his mother would at home. She was not so different from Jack. In the same ways predictable. He knew Jack would check that they had left things as they had found them, even if the hose had been tangled on the ground when they arrived. The reality of the world didn't matter as much as his vision of it. Perhaps that was a religious way of seeing the world. It definitely was, Santiago thought a moment later, remembering that his mother had been raised Christian, even though she no longer was.

Santiago avoided the pits of water around the truck and found Matthew staring into the trunk, thumb in mouth, stunned. There was a cluster of flies marooned on the pale islands of his feet, dark stains spread across the front of his shorts like pee. Santiago climbed into the trunk and handed Matthew two of the fold-up chairs, hoping Matthew could feel the love in how carefully he passed him the bundles, and hauled the other two over his shoulder. The blue cooler with the white lid they would carry together. He wanted to tell Matthew about the time last summer when he'd found a dog and a cat fighting in the parking lot of his building. The cat brandished its teeth, and its tail in the air whipped forward and back. The dog was twice its size, huffing and barking loudly, trying to fake the cat out by lunging on its front paws without really attacking. Santiago knew what he had to do; he swept the cat off the ground and wrapped his arms around it, pressing it to his chest, already imagining how he would tell his mother he had saved a helpless creature. She would be proud of him. The cat flailed, its legs kicking loose from his arms, until finally, it sunk its teeth into his forearm. The two pale circles were still there, on the inside of his left arm, above the wrist. He held his side of the cooler higher, bearing a larger share of the weight, thinking of what his mother would do. In this way, the love he had for Matthew was like that his mother had for him, made in the same shape. He loved Matthew as if he were part of himself, making his love felt through sacrifices and sufferings that would go unnoticed, but that made all the difference.

Through the opening in the wall of trees, they found sun-bleached picnic tables and prehistoric grills scattered under the dappled shade of tall trees. Santiago had the sense of witnessing something private, as if the walls had vanished around each family in the rooms the palms and shrubs made around them. It thrilled him, to watch, to eavesdrop, to glimpse how other people lived when they thought no one was watching.

In one room, a father with a hand wrapped around the neck of a beer danced bachata in front of the grill as the smoke enveloped him, full of

66    light. His wife was shaking her head from side to side, laughing at his antics, how he danced as if the ground would burn his feet if he kept still. She put out paper plates and plastic utensils on the picnic table for the hot dogs, smiling over a bowl of sliced oranges. There were two shirtless boys, who looked like miniatures of their father, either seven or eight. They ran around swinging branches at each other, kicking themselves from the tree trunks and yelling like samurais. The girl, who must have been sixteen, had a flourish of pale stretch marks above the hemline of her pink sundress. She sat with her back to the food spread across the picnic table, fanning herself with a paper plate folded in half between her fingers. Her voice was loud and plaintive, magnetic and needy, cooing *mami* and *papi*, as she complained about the sun and her brothers and the hot dogs burning on the grill—Santiago watched her, occupying her life like a stage. He was spellbound. What would it be like to grow up like this, with both of his parents, with a brother that wasn't many years older than him and from a different marriage? What would it be like to go on camping trips with his own family? If he weren't a guest? Would he coo? Would he holler and yell? Would he take up all the space he imagined taking up in his head?

He was reminded of a story, one of his brother's tales, from when he was a toddler. They were in the finca of some relative for his birthday, with all of the family. Everyone was drinking, eating, and dancing, and so it wasn't until hours later, once they lit the three candles on the cake for Santiago that they realized he was missing. They searched for him under every cot and bed, in every cabinet and closet, in every bathroom and shed, even in the chicken coop and the stable. The melodramas spilled out from the aunties and girl cousins searching the fruit trees around the house, holding onto their skirts. Perhaps the guerillas had taken him. Or perhaps a snake or spider had gotten to him. Perhaps he had fallen down a well, into a pool, or in the river. His brother was the hero who found him, hours later, in the middle of a field across the house. Somehow he'd gotten past the barbed wire and nestled himself beside a cow asleep on its side. He had known nature, but forgotten it, was the lesson he took from the story. In Miami, his mother and brother would've never gone camping during a free weekend, because they, too, had forgotten nature. They would have gone to the mall or a restaurant. The beach, only if he begged them, but never in the water, no matter what he said. Then they would come back home, retreat into their separate rooms to watch television or call Colombia. This trip to Naples—or *nipples,* as Matthew said it—was another thing in his collection of things that made him different from his mother and brother, which these days, was reason enough for doing anything.

"What you looking at?" the girl in the pink sundress snapped at him, shooing him away like a stray dog with her paper plate. "This ain't no show."

At the jolt of her voice, Santiago almost screamed. He felt incredibly visible, as if he gave off light. He never could tell when he was and wasn't seen. Without looking at her, he mouthed *sorry,* the sound caught in his throat. He turned to Matthew as if he'd spoken something important just then, and his expression must have shown his pain, or embarrassment, because what he saw was Matthew's face, from one moment to the next, shed its seriousness. It was like the sped-up videos they watched in science class, a field of yellow tulips opening their petals. "You're already making friends," Matthew said, punching his shoulder and knocking something out of place. In a moment, laughter spilled from his mouth.

The campsites branched out from the dirt path like more private rooms. Recessed in the trees were sleek tents catching the sun like tin, camping chairs arranged in circles around ashen pits, and large dogs lapping water from plastic pails. He was reminded of the corridors of the first building in Miami he had lived in, each apartment door jammed

68 open by a chancla or newspaper, each living room bared for him to imagine a life in. With the same dangerous curiosity, he looked into the campsites they passed now. He could have been anyone else, if only the world were different by a degree or an inch, by the distance his brother had caught between his fingers one night not so long ago—if only. He almost forget what he was doing, when Talia and Jack came into view. The sun laid in a crisp, golden sheet over them and he remembered that he didn't want another life. Matthew dropped his side of the cooler on the ground; Santiago dragged it by himself the rest of the way. This, the family that took him every other weekend his mother worked back-to-back shifts. The family that took him now that his brother couldn't be trusted. That loved him like family. This was his.

"Preciosos," Talia said. "Como hermanos." She waved them together with the black disposable camera in her hands, her bracelets clinking up and down her forearm. Santiago lined his back up with Matthew's, their heads together. Matthew pushed back with his skull and he pushed back with his, slippery with sweat. He laughed, tasting the salt on his lips, smelling the earth that clung to his body. He held the pose, the smile, the illusion of being brothers. Talia said Jack's name in a whine, sucked her lips, and dragged him by the arm from the patch of ground he was sweeping clear with his feet for the tent. He stood behind them, his arms reaching beyond their shoulders, thumbs up on both hands. The three of them stared ahead, at Talia.

"Whiskey," she said, snapping the picture without giving them a chance to finish the "-key."

What a woman, Santiago thought. She had collected the three of them, brought them together as her family. But how? It was she who was at their center, where he wanted to be, where one day he hoped to find himself, with these men or others. He loved his mother, but he wondered what it would be like if she were more like Talia, who was soft, feminine, smiling—not like a woman trying to be both mother and father, he thought, feeling shame and guilt and pity all at once. He wrapped his arms around Matthew's shoulders, angry at himself for having thought bad of his mother. Talia noticed. Thinking he was posing for another picture, she crouched to get them from a lower angle this time. Jack lowered his head, his shadow spreading and deepening over them, as he inserted himself again. Another picture was snapped.

"Don't get too cozy," said Jack, gripping their shoulders and shaking them in the way that made Santiago feel like the floor was falling out beneath him.

"Are they not adorable?" Talia said, to herself, to the air, because Jack wasn't the kind of man who found anything adorable, and in a moment, she flew, laughing, hanging over Jack's shoulder like a sack of rice.

"Let those boys get to work, woman."

Santiago noticed the sweat smeared on his forearms, belonging to either Matthew or Jack, the thin black hairs on them in disarray, and ran his arms across his face, feeling less alone.

The campfire crackled like in the movies. Smoldering flecks rose above the flames, but disappeared into the night without getting too far. His skin mesmerized him, the way the oranges deepened into red and then lightened into yellow, and all the colors in between that he had no name for. Everyone else, with their heads bowed to the fire, glowed like he did. Around them, the darkness of the forest had become boundless and complete, almost solid, like the silence. They prayed before every meal and before bed. The first night he had stayed with them, he'd returned from brushing his teeth to find Jack flanked by Matthew and Talia, all three knelt at the side of the bunk bed in Matthew's room. It took him a moment to realize what they were doing. He didn't know if he was supposed to join them or if they had begun without him on purpose. He had sat at Matthew's right and looked over the curve of his

70 cheeks, at the profile of Jack with his long, quivering lashes, and Talia with her full lips moving silently over private words. Then as now, Jack said "Amen," and Talia and Matthew followed, and without thinking, he said it, too, though he had been looking at them the entire time.

They ate the way Jack liked, without speaking. Each mouth moved over the aluminum foil pouches unfolded across their laps, the pieces of pale fish sitting in pools of juice. Talia had also prepared roasted yams and sweet plantains that morning. The groans came from Jack, from somewhere inside of him, sounds of tremendous pleasure and relief. She always cooked his favorite foods, and after every meal she'd ask if he'd been reminded of home. She never made arepas or tamales or anything resembling Venezuelan food.

When somewhere nearby a boombox belted out, Jack flinched. If there were a table he would have flipped it. There were bottles clinking and people laughing, and Santiago felt the pleasure he always felt, as earlier with the flies, of watching Jack inconvenienced by what he couldn't control of the world. Santiago hummed with the music, low enough that he could feel the rhythm thrumming through his tongue and throat without anyone hearing him. He stopped just as the song finished and started again with the new one. It was the only way he could eat this food he hated. That was the last song, he thought after each song returned them to silence. He looked around the campfire at Matthew sitting on the ground between his mother's legs eating the plantains with his fingers, and Talia plucking the bones from Matthew's fish so he would eat his portion, and Jack sitting by himself across the fire unfolding a second aluminum bundle over his first. The silence each song left behind felt final and bleak only to him. He looked out at the twitching darkness below the trees. Somewhere out there were people having fun. Enjoying life. He wanted to be with them. When a new song boomed out, the joy he felt was so vivid he could almost see the music spreading through the darkness, a wave of brilliant colors.

"You boys better eat quick and get to bed," Jack said, as he spit a mouthful of bones into the fire. He could parse them from the fish with his tongue, collecting them in his cheek without effort. "Tomorrow will be an early one."

Matthew gathered his legs below him and turned around to face Talia. His eyes made a silent appeal to her. When she said nothing, he stood up and sat back down next to Santiago in the chair he'd left empty since they gathered around the fire. Matthew smirked at him, like he had a secret plan in mind. He let their knees touch, and instinctively, Santiago nodded, letting himself be recruited to Matthew's side. He'd noticed before, how Matthew moved from him to Talia, from one allegiance to the other. Perhaps their whole friendship was an elaborate means to piss off Jack. Perhaps everyone saw this except for him. He looked around the fire at the uncomfortable silence. He shouldn't think this way, Santiago told himself. He didn't like it when paranoid thoughts raced through his head like this, so much like being with his mother.

"This is really good," Santiago said to Jack across the fire. The truth was he hated the fish. He mashed every morsel between his fingers until it was a flakey white mound before putting it in his mouth. He was too shy to say anything about it, or to ask Talia to pluck the bones like she did with Matthew's. He imagined a needle lodged in his throat if he wasn't thorough and missed one. How it would feel. But he found himself saying these things he didn't mean, these lies, because he wanted Jack to know that if he were Matthew he would love him no matter how difficult he was as a father. Jack was enough.

"At least I have one grateful boy," said Jack. He wiped the grease from his lips on the back of his hand and stood up. He made his way around the fire toward Talia—they all watched him—and awkwardly, as if it were a decision made last minute, he ran his hand through

Santiago's hair. Such firm, terrifying pressure. Santiago felt each finger rake across his scalp, even after Jack had left him and moved onto Talia. Jack kissed her behind the ear, then on the cheek from the other side, bending her head from one side to the other with the force of his love. She didn't stop him. She let herself be kissed. She arched her head this way and that, opening up patches of her skin that needed to be kissed. At some point his own mother and father had been the same way, two adults kissing in front of a fire, in love, though it was hard to imagine. Santiago had no memories of them together and his brother always asked "Who?" when he asked for a story with his father. The one photograph he had was wedged into the corner of a cork board in his bedroom. It was of him and his father somewhere with a pool, the water behind them a blue jewel. They sat under a roof, just the two of them. On his father's lap, he smiled with all his teeth—a smile he didn't smile anymore—and his father grinned behind him, that grin that made his lips curl up at one side and reveal the crescents of his yellowed teeth. His father stared ahead, his eyes circled by the black metal frames of his glasses, unaware that one day he would be separated from his only son. That was how he remembered his father, just as he was in that picture, in front of that pool and under that roof—without his mother or brother—and unaware of the future. Whenever he imagined the house his brother spoke of, he never knew where to place his father, in which room, with what household prop in his hands, even if for a time the four of them had lived together. It was shocking to think that his father had been central to his mother and brother's stories and that if he were asked to describe his father, he would only be able to describe that one picture, his fragment of the whole piece. He was ashamed of how little he knew of it all.

Jack's long black fingers crawled over Talia's head like spiders, stumbling down her shoulders, then her arms, kneading circles where they stepped. She let out whimpers that sounded escaped, as if she were trying to hold them back but failed. He was taking her away from them; she was letting herself be taken. His own mother had promised she would never bring another man near him and his brother until they were both grown, a promise he hadn't asked for or entirely comprehended—a promise he now understood she'd made for herself. It was like her willful silence on their past, more for her than for him. He respected her choices.

"Go on now. Shower," Jack said without lifting his mouth from her skin.

The openness of their love put Santagio in a mood, such that walking to the restrooms he held onto Matthew's arm near his armpit, that damp field of heat, thinking about consuming him with his mouth, though he was sure his best friend was thinking about something else, like soccer or death.

Matthew wrestled his arm away.

"Not now," he said.

They found the tent standing. Inside were two inflatable beds and between them their backpacks. They made the bed and sat in their underwear, sharing a box of raisins and playing a card game Matthew made up as they went. Talia asked Santiago if he wanted to call his mother, and he realized he hadn't thought of her in hours. She answered almost immediately and he stepped out of the tent to tell her about the day. She laughed when she heard about the flies. She said she was in his bed and that she had eaten dinner by herself since his brother was out again. He wandered away from the camp as he listened to her. A cool breeze came and went around his ankles. The gravel crunched beneath his feet like a sheet of ice. Lanterns and flashlights from other camps glowed across the dark in orbs. Crickets and other bugs he didn't know cried and he could swear he'd lived this moment before—in another life—in a dream last week—in Colombia. He kept walking. He heard footsteps and laughter nearby, and turned to see Talia and Jack with towels slung over their shoulders, on their way to the showers, and they went on without seeing him, groping each other in the dark. If they had another child, would Matthew become like his own half-brother, embittered, like a domestic animal thrown in a cage and let loose in the wild? His mother was talking, and when he noticed he made an effort to pay attention. He almost said he was sorry but she hadn't noticed. A cousin of his in Colombia was sick. She was sending money so that they would take him to a private hospital. Someone had misread his prescription at the public clinic and was giving him ten times as much medicine. He was now breaking out in hives all over, even under his tongue, between his buttcheeks. Even on his balls, she said. "Can you imagine?" Something in her voice pushed him back again. Santiago fought the urge to hang up on her immediately and be through with the call. If everyone in Colombia died, he would be happy. She wouldn't have to work as hard anymore. She could spend time with him and his brother, keep them together—and thinking so he wished everyone dead. He decided not to call her tomorrow.

When he got back to the tent, Matthew was splayed on his stomach, with his arms circled around his head as he always slept. Santiago lowered himself onto the air mattress, aware of every part of his body, as if one thoughtless movement could rip apart the tent. They had never slept side-by-side since Matthew had a bunk bed that Jack had gotten from the church, on which they slept stacked on top of each other, together but separate. Santiago left a few inches between their bodies now, his arm hanging off the mattress and his leg running along the seam. The sheets already smelled warm and sweet. He wanted more of it, more of the rush and vertigo the smell gave him, like he was creeping to the edge of himself and staring down a precipice. He could have more of it.

He could close his eyes and roll over. He could touch Matthew with all of himself, and it would be perfectly normal, even tender. Talia would even think so when she and Jack returned from the showers. She might even take a picture with her camera.

With his eyes closed, he pretended to sleep when Talia and Jack returned. He could hear Talia running her head through the towel, Jack stepping into fresh briefs, the floor crinkling below them like grocery bags. And for a moment he even felt their eyes rest on him and Matthew with something like pride, or love, before the light went out. In the dark, he kept his eyes shut. They hadn't prayed together tonight, and now, alone, he wished he wouldn't fall asleep yet or ever. His hand probed the distance that separated him from Matthew, an inch or two in which he could feel the heat his body gave off. Finally, when he opened his eyes, everything looked lunar and colossal in shades of gray. He didn't move under the weight of his body stretching out from him like a landscape, like a world apart from the boy he loved. He thanked God for Matthew.

Scraps of blues and grays assembled themselves in Jack's outline, towering above him. A hand was pressed over his mouth and another pinned his arm down to the mattress.

Santiago thought of his mother as his breath filled the space between his lips and Jack's hand, when she whispered into his ear *You're my treasure* and *I would die if something happened to you*, that weekend, many weekends ago, that she let him sleep over at Matthew's house for the first time. He could tell his mother about Jack, about all those mornings he woke them before sunrise with some unnecessary task. How one weekend, there was a bootcamp in the backyard he'd set up by moonlight. A barbed wire tunnel they had to crawl under with only their elbows as the first birds sung over their heads. A rope tied between the mango trees they had to cross like monkeys as Jack threatened them with the hose. He could tell her of how every Sunday he woke them before sunrise to wash the van so that it sparkled brighter than any other in the church parking lot. He could tell his mother about any other of Jack's so-called Boy's Missions. He could—and he made the choice not to. Jack let him go when he read the obedience in his eyes. Almost immediately, Santiago missed the leathery surface of the palm cupped over his mouth, and those long fingers bracing his cheek with a pressure that had both frightened and comforted him. Jack woke Matthew in the same way and the air mattress jumped like a trampoline when he stood up. That was the way the world was, Santiago thought, as his body bounced to the center of the bed, up against Matthew's, with a joy that fizzed.

Even with his neck bent, Jack grazed the top of the tent with his head. The whites of his eyes blinked in and out of the darkness like fireflies above them. He mimed jamming his feet into shoes and tying the laces with swift tugs. In the other bed, Talia still slept with her arms crossed over her chest like a mummy. Jack nodded at the world beyond the tent and something of the gesture told them that the clock was ticking.

The headlights of the van singled out a row of trees. Matthew took the backseat and Santiago walked across the yellow beams to the other side on his tiptoes like a ballerina crossing her imaginary stage in front of her audience. He looked from door to door, realizing he could sit in the back with Matthew or up front with Jack.

He took Talia's place.

"Open up that lunchbox at your feet," said Jack. Inside of the blue pouch were two protein bars, two bananas, and a large water bottle. Matthew looked down at the provisions Santiago passed him as if he'd forgotten how to eat. Just eat it, Santiago tried to say with his eyes, but Matthew looked through him. His mouth was still sticky with sleep when he asked why his mother wasn't coming.

"This is a Boy's Mission," said Jack. He bent his arm behind Santiago's seat to reverse out of the parking spot. "Now eat."

They left the campgrounds through the same road. The digital clock on the dashboard said ten past five. Santiago turned the radio to Jack's station and adjusted the volume until Jack was satisfied. They weren't supposed to talk while the radio was on, especially if it was a pastor going on about how God controlled every move their lives made. He thought suddenly of his mother. She never took them to church. There were no crosses on the walls of their house or Bibles at their bedside. When had she stopped needing a God? She would be awake by now, heating an arepa over the blue flames of the stove and listening to Caracol Colombia on the radio. She wanted more than God could give her. She wanted more than what satisfied Jack. Who was happier? Santiago asked himself, watching Jack's face in relief and thinking of his mother. Jack seemed in control of his world, at least. He imposed his vision so ruthlessly and rightously that it was like a trap they had all fallen into, and out of which they knew no way out. Santiago almost looked forward to it, the unnecessary struggle, the shouted commands, and the threat of violence—they were nothing like the passiveness of his mother, who would now be dumping the rest of her coffee in the sink and hurrying off to work. Like a chicken without its head, his brother had said, in the same way he repeated everything else he overheard, stumbling through the phrase. His mother hadn't been able to hold on to his father, or their homeland, or even his brother. She had a vision only she could see, and what use was that?

Jack pulled over a short drive from the campground. He parked on the shoulder of the road and hopped the wooden fence led by the beam of his flashlight. Since there was no obvious path, they made their own, Jack passing the branches to Matthew, and Matthew to Santiago, so that they were like a small dispatch of ants burrowing through new territory.



77

78 His senses sharpened with alarm, fearing how little he could see and how much he could imagine. Around them, animals fled, crushing branches below their feet. Only the birds in the trees held their stations. He could hear at least three different kinds. One, like an alarm clock, sang the same disturbing note without stopping. Another sang a scale of notes, sweeping upward every few seconds, its call answered from somewhere near by another bird. The last, louder than all the others, cawed a single, brief note, whose echo haunted the song of all the others. When Matthew snickered, Santiago felt frivolous for trying to find comfort in the bird songs, as if his mind had been read, although it was impossible. Matthew could not read his mind, he must think that, he told himself. It was just Matthew doing what came naturally to him, making fun of the world around him, as if he would be happy to start again in another world.

Past a felled trunk covered in moon-bright mushrooms, the branches came apart, opening up onto a dirt road large enough for a small car. The sky came into view, a pale, silvery sheet of blue moving like water between the banks of canopy. "Look," Jack whispered. His flashlight shot off into the trees. He stopped them behind the span of his arms. An iguana stretched across the road, not more than ten feet away. It was doing push-ups though its arms were those of a frail, old man, and for a moment it was funny before Santiago realized that the animal was alive and real. Breaths quivered through the layers of skin that hung like a bib around its neck. Dim yellow spikes along the curve of its head flared up and down, as if catching a wind, and its eyes flickered from one direction to another, wildly, as it considered routes of escape. Santiago looked back at the wall of trees they had come from. He could no longer see the passage they had taken. All the trees flung themselves in the same dark, identical way. Even the felled trunk, when he looked for it, was two, three, possibly four different ones. In a moment, Matthew rushed toward the iguana in a sprint, flapping his arms and hollering like a rooster. The reptile ran across the path, disappeared, and to Santiago's surprise, Jack laughed. Here was Matthew, fearless in the face of an obstacle, bold and stupid—that was something Jack could appreciate. Without the iguana, there was no distinction between either side of the road. They turned right, following Jack. There was no way to guess what Jack saw, what compelled him to bring them here, but at least Jack knew where they were going, and this thought comforted Santiago as he reached the same conclusion he had hundreds of times before: there were just some things in the world that he couldn't understand.

The beam of the flashlight faded as the world lit up. Jack pointed out the red triangles nailed to the tree trunks, looking over his shoulder, past Matthew, at Santiago, as if he were the one that needed to hear this. "The triangles stay where they're nailed," said Jack, "because the trees grow upward from their branches, not their trunks. In a year, when we come back, the trees will be taller, but the triangles will be in the same place."

"This is what you two need," he continued, "not to be coddled the way your mothers do. You need to be ready to take care of them when the time comes. You'll never know when the time comes. It'll come by surprise and either you'll fail them or you won't."

Neither one of them responded. Jack didn't say anything more. They continued to walk under the trees. The silence bound them. Santiago put his hand on Matthew's shoulder blade. *I love you, I love you.* He hoped the message would pass silently through his fingers. He felt a fear he'd had before, that he needed the people in his life more than they needed him. This fear made him want to be useful and polite, so that no one would ever tire of him, the way he noticed some people drained those around them. Like his brother, he thought, like his mother. Like his father. And then the fear roared inside of him, and he saw the problem from a different angle, in a different light. He had to care less about people. He had to separate himself from others, let them need and miss him. But of course, there was nothing to him more exhausting than trying not to care. It was always an effort. He pulled his touch from Matthew. The shape of his hand clung to the fabric like a ghost.

He had no clue how much time had passed when they stopped at a fork in the road. Holding his neck up felt like an enormous effort. The heat weighed on him. It was as if they were underwater. The sun cut sharp, dazzling shapes in the canopy.

"So what are we doing boys? Are we going long or short?"

Despite reading the signposts—one mile versus seven—Santiago had no clue what they meant. The most he had ever walked was at the mall.

"Long," said Santiago. It was the right answer, the answer Jack wanted. Matthew glared at him with his own unanswered question: *Why can't you be quiet now, like you always are?*

After the fork, the sparse trees became dense. The branches swept his shoulders like waxy feathers. Nature ran out on either side of him into a darkness pierced through by threads of light. He could have said no, turned back, but he waited. He wanted to prove to Jack that he could work through the overwhelming fear roiling inside of him. That for him, fear was like a math problem that could be taken apart and solved with enough thinking. The wind came and went, combing the branches. A mirage deepened and spread ahead of them, sparkling like a mirror in the distance. He hadn't worked through his fear as much as he had committed to it when he realized it was too late to turn back. The path ended abruptly at the shore of a swamp. It hadn't been a mirage at all. The mangroves, the only tree he knew the name of, stood on their roots above the brown water, their understory streaked with lurking shadows. Winged insects patrolled the edge of the water. Tadpoles festered in the shallows.

"Jesus Christ," Jack said, turning to them. He looked past them, down the narrow path in the trees they had come from. "Wait here."



He returned a moment later with a branch that was almost as long as his legs, a staff for a wizard. He tightened the shoelaces of his boots and without saying anything else, he entered the water. The brown murk flung itself away from his body and then raced back towards his legs, like it recognized him.

"This is a Boy's Mission," he shouted. "We don't tell anyone about this."

Matthew entered next with his arms out in front of him, not knowing what to do with them as the water reached up his waist.

Santiago looked down at the water, his heart stilled. There was no telling what lurked below the surface of his own face, reflected. The water swallowed him next. Under his soles, the floor sunk as he imagined quicksand would and he hurried into the next step, thrashing into the water with his chest. He found that his shoes and shorts, soaked, became impossibly heavy, like in the nightmares in which he was being chased, and where try as he did to run, his legs were heavy as lead.

Ahead of them, Jack prodded the water with the staff to frighten away whatever awaited their next steps. His legs breaking through the water, that churning sound, dredged from Santiago's mind a fragment of a memory—less memory than an image—of women washing clothes by hand. The image came and went and he was left with a desire to be home. In Colombia or in Miami. It didn't matter. The airport the day they left could have been the scene of a funeral. Everyone clutched each other's faces and cried. He wanted to go back to Colombia; he put the words together for the first time. He wanted to have the attention and love his mother had for this place he didn't know. He waited for something to touch his legs below water, for a snake to wrap around his hips and drag him away. Would Jack and Matthew even notice, he

82 asked himself, and if they did, how far would they go to save him. He grabbed the back of Matthew's shirt in his fist. Matthew's shoulders rose then shivered in response, with surprise or disgust, as he registered the shock. Santiago wouldn't let go. He would drag Matthew with him. They would die together.

There was no end to the water ahead of them. Matthew turned around, his face was saying, *I'm sorry*, and Santiago realized for the first time that they were in real danger. He really was cold and wet. He latched his fingers around Matthew's elbow. His hand squeezed down his arm until he held Matthew's hand below the water. He wanted to protect Matthew from Jack, Jack who was his stepfather, Jack who would after this weekend, if they made it through this day, continue to be in Matthew's life, for as long as they could all foresee. By Sunday evening, Santiago would be back with his own mother and brother, in their nicer apartment, where they kept the A/C below seventy-four and where there were more than ten channels on the television. Where there was no tyrant or law. This was only temporary for him, but for Matthew it was life.

As the other shore came into view, Santiago didn't expect the emptiness that opened inside of him. It was a morning he would never forget and like most such moments, he tried to commit it all to memory while it lived. He tried to record in his mind how his fingers twined with Matthew's felt, the color of the water and how far up his stomach it reached, but he soon thought of the airport again, the crying, the clutching of faces and bodies, flashes of all of his brother's stories racing through his head, and he knew that this moment in the swamp would be like that, nothing, except for the fewest details that were caught and kept, and that would, throughout the rest of his life, be dredged up from his memory. He no longer wanted to make it to the other side. He wanted to die, just once, just now, here.

The sun was slumped behind the trees when they reached the camp. The smell rising to his nose from his shirt was ripe and green. He had never smelled like this before, and now he knew that he could. That was enough for him. He didn't care anymore if Jack or Matthew liked him, if they even thought about him. He would behave like they did, detached from everything outside of themselves, lost inside of their heads. He marched past Talia, straight to the bathroom, leaving her head mid-swing toward Jack. He showered, washed his hair with the bar of soap left in the stall by someone before him. The water was icy, coming out in spurts, and his skin tightened, tingling, until he felt nothing at all.

The knock on the door startled him. He had stood there senseless, how long he didn't know. He would stay there until the weekend was over. He hadn't brought a towel.

Below the door, the two pale feet in the leather sandals belonged to Matthew. Santiago clenched his fists at his side, digging his knuckles into his thighs for something below the skin, something that would spill out with exactly what he had to say and do now. He slid the lock open and pushed the door open an inch, enough space for Matthew's fingers to reach through. He cupped his penis, the pruned sack small in his hands. He was crying silently.

Matthew entered the stall and stepped out of his shorts and underwear, one tangle of clothes flung over the door of the stall, with such ease and confidence and a slap. His arms circled Santiago's waist, Santiago's circled his neck. They stood together, bones trembling. They were still caught in the swamp, submerged to their waists in dark water, waiting for Jack to explain to them what had compelled him, waiting for something to drag them into the unseen world below the surface. &<

..............................................................................................................

*Santiago José Sánchez is a writer and photographer currently studying at the Iowa Writers' Workshop and has been published in* Subtropics, Joyland, *and* Mask Magazine.

# SYMPTOMS OF MANHOOD

## JOHN SIBLEY WILLIAMS

I am trying to tell you something
but the fire in my mouth has lost its
oxygen. I am all unstruck flint &
lost potential. & I'm no good at this
settling for beauty. Anxious animals
pour from the tree line into the cross
–hairs & I am trying to tell you I am
more than the men before me. Yes,
I plant my feet firm & as unreliable;
but just this once I'll try to hold you
how a doe holds the forest in place.
Dead, dying, or free, for now, how a
doe holds, is held by what it holds.

# THAN A SPEEDING BULLET

## JOHN SIBLEY WILLIAMS

Anything can be mistaken for people:
skyscraper, burning silo, a whole city
busy neglecting itself, a river scarred
over in ice. From up here, red cape
weighing down the wings it gives,
it's hard to tell if the world is swelling
or swallowing, if life is just a costume
we take off & put back on without
warmth. Before my brother flew
a bit too high to steer home safely,
he'd cut up the curtains & wrap me
in barkcloth & push my ten-year-old
body off our one-story roof, saying
*the sky never stops calling us*. I still
can't remember the how of my landing,
if my ankle eventually untwisted,
if our father ever unwore his anger.
But there was a moment, mid-ascent
or mid-fall, this gentle ratio of land to
sky seemed sustainable. Before he
ransacked his veins with heaven, before
I tried & tried & failed to join him there,
there was a moment I thought the sky
filled with justice, that guilt like all duties
could be hurdled in a single bound.

# SALINAS

## JOHN SIBLEY WILLIAMS

Miles pass. Breaths. Landscapes scorch
by the window. Upturned faces everywhere

hunting for rain. Lettuce, wild vines, insects
& the things that eat them. Undocumented

work going on in the deepest
recesses of summer.

The smell of machines, ungreased levers
working each other up into whine.

A horse on the horizon. A jangle of belled goats. Thirst.

Hands, their splitting.

Our headlights stay on all day
to remind us to see.

Nothing says *stay*.
Nothing has to.

We are pulled in too many directions
to make a home of things.

Proof that we were ever here is already disappearing.

*John Sibley Williams's most recent books are* As One Fire Consumes Another *(Orison Poetry Prize) and* Skin Memory *(University of Nebraska Press/Backwaters Prize). He lives in Oregon.*

# BEAUTY & THE BEASTLY

DEBORA KUAN

Desire is the flaw of the hungry, and if
you are a woman, you
cannot be hungry. Instead you may
crimp your bite-marks on the gilded
bathroom mirror, or
cinch the linen napkin through its ring

to your face, which is where he has
built his castle. There, there,
you live with him, just the two of you,
only a year of cold sheet between.
You are free, yet he keeps you
whole, a dimpled bowl of

snow interred in an ice-box
to bring out in summer
to applause. To surround. Yet
what is more implausible: the moat
surrounding your new house, or
the beast, a moat surrounding a man?

Don't answer. Look, there,
in the mirror, you are learning.
A lesson of heat forms a bubble, then pops:
A man only need be forgiven. A woman
must prove she can even love
what kills her.

# INTENTIONS

## DEBORA KUAN

Six months pregnant, I go to the eyeglass shop
to tighten the corners of my glasses—

but the man who attempts to help me
snaps off one wing by mistake

and cannot reattach the hinge.
With apology, he returns

my life to me, and I hold it
in my hands, a crippled sparrow.

Lunchtime faces near and recede—
plates of melted custard,

a Pissarro of emphatic chatter—
as I retrace the way I came,

fledgling slow, a glass piano
on the floor of the sea,

my body braced for
whatever softness I shall meet.

Debora Kuan's most recent poetry collection is Lunch Portraits (Brooklyn Arts Press). Her poetry and fiction have appeared in The Baffler, The New Republic, Boston Review, and other publications.

# ALABAMA FUNERAL

KRISTEN ISKANDRIAN

The sitter arrived with a Ziploc bag of brightly colored string.

"For friendship bracelets," she said, one eye veering off.

"Yes," Bette said. The sitter's eye was particularly lazy today; Bette had never gotten used to it, although she herself, when extra tired, had an eye prone to drifting. Bette was aware that she could be, in a multitude of ways, a perfect hypocrite.

She was named after Bette Midler, which had always embarrassed her, so she told people she was named after Bette Davis. "So it's 'Betty'?" people would ask, and then she'd have to correct them, and they'd be confused, wondering why anyone would name someone after the spelling of one person's name and the pronunciation of another's. *That's their problem*, Bette would think to herself.

A large Domino's pizza was on the kitchen table. Bette pulled paper plates down from the pantry.

"Try for an eight o'clock bedtime. Liesl can stay up and read if she wants." Liesl was named after Liesl von Trapp, obviously. "Don't let George have any candy. He'll beg you for it and tell you that I said it was okay. It's not okay. I'll be upset if he has any, and I'll be able to tell. I can always tell."

George was named after any George except George Bush. Bette had always liked the name, the round squish of it in her mouth.

She called the kids upstairs to say goodbye. Liesl was twelve and resented having a babysitter, in very much the same way that Liesl von Trapp pouted about being too old to have a governess. One day, Bette told her, you are going to get locked out of the house in the rain after dancing in a gazebo with your Hitler Youth boyfriend and after you shimmy up the drain pipe and get changed into dry clothes you will be so happy that a babysitter was here to cover for you.

Whatever, Liesl had said. We don't even have a gazebo.

"Be good. Be helpful. George—no candy." She kissed them near their ears, whispering *I love you* ferociously into them.

✢   ✢   ✢

On the floor of the backseat of the minivan were deviled eggs and pineapple casserole. The reason she drove a minivan was because she always assumed that she and Andrew would have three kids, and all the stuff and friends that three kids would accumulate. But she'd had three pregnancies and only two kids. Math was cruel to her as a child and continued to be cruel, she felt, staring in her rearview mirror at the rows of empty seats as she pulled out of the driveway.

But she didn't mind throwing people off. Where were the rest of her children? Or, for that matter, more recently, where *was* Andrew? "I love having extra space," she would say. "For groceries, or if I see a coffee table on the side of the road." She would never pick up someone's cast-off furniture, but not everyone knew this about her. She seemed like the type of person who might. Often she imagined the bouncing and rattling of the unfilled car as the echo of her empty womb, and it comforted her, even as it pained her.

Gold with leather seats, seat warmers, lane-merge sensors, a generous back-up camera—it was one of few material possessions that she really, truly loved. She went for all the extras, the deluxe package.

Generally extras when it came to cars depressed her, because something that cost $1,000 more would, in next year's model, be included in the base price. But the extravagance had felt necessary, urgent, even.



She'd bought the car after securing a big client at work. Technically the money went into a shared bank account and was both of theirs, but she made more than Andrew, and it was her name on the bill of sale. Prior to the minivan she'd driven a Honda Civic, which could just barely fit the two car seats in the back, and definitely wouldn't have room for a third, which was a longstanding part of the plan.

What about an SUV, Andrew, who drove a Yaris, had suggested.

But Bette hated SUVs. She felt they were for people who didn't know what kind of people they were.

I'm very comfortable driving a minivan, she'd said.

It's kind of cool, Andrew had said. Sort of low-key ironic. But you can make anything cool.

Thank you, she'd said, but I have come to loathe irony.

Still, she'd been flattered by the compliment, and thinking about it now, she wished she'd told him that at the time, instead of trampling it, which was her instinct, and one she rarely suppressed.

Bette drove out of the neighborhood just as the streetlights turned on. Late February had been warm, but now it was early March and chilly. She'd forgotten to bring the plants on the porch inside before the cold snap, and when she remembered it probably would not have been too late, but by that point she felt she'd sealed their fate, and had accepted their deaths, and felt more than a tinge of relief. She disliked watering them; she disliked how she was constantly forgetting and then re-remembering them. She didn't like to admit that she was the kind of person who'd willingly let plants die, but in the scheme of things, over the course of a life, of all the many truths people were obliged to admit about themselves, she figured it wasn't the worst.

*    *    *

The funeral party had been Walter's idea. Walter was a half-friend, one of those Bette could forget about when he wasn't immediately in front of her, but never an unwelcome face in a crowd. She'd started to treasure those ones more than the full-friends, with their demands and constant exhortations to get together, to keep in touch. Exhausting. Walter had a vision: to convene a group of people, each of whom would have signed up to bring one to two Southern funeral dishes from the cult favorite cookbook *Being Dead Is No Excuse*, with the result being an odd assemblage that might mimic an actual funeral. Guests would be encouraged to share stories of loss, casual eulogies, cooking tips, whatever the chemistry of the evening moved them to disclose. Both of Walter's parents were dead and he missed them with a child's missing, fondly and frequently referring to them as *Mama* and *Daddy*. It was for them that he conceived of the whole thing. *I've wanted to do this for a long time*, the emailed invitation read, with a link to Sign Up Genius where guests were to submit what they would be contributing. By the time Bette had clicked on it, only the eggs (*sweet stuffed*, also known in some Mississippi circles as *peckerwood*) and the pineapple casserole were left.

Walter answered the door in a dark suit. His tie seemed extra wide. Andrew always favored skinny ties; of course he did. For the briefest moment Bette forgot where she was. The feeling washed over her—*nooo make it stop, no, no*—her life a thing utterly alien and dismal—then passed just as quickly.

"Well, don't you look beautiful. Let me take those from you." He reached for the foil-wrapped Pyrex dishes.

A woman sat at the upright piano playing jazz standards. Walter handed Bette a coupe of champagne and introduced her to a man who looked exactly, disconcertingly, like a perfect combination of Chuck

Norris and Vincent van Gogh, as he would be drawn by Chuck Close. *93*
His pores were prominent enough to make Bette suddenly self-conscious
about her own.

"Bette, this is Blake, an artist. Blake, this is Bette, a—wonderful
woman of many talents."

"I'm a copywriter," Bette said, slurping from her overly full glass.
Some champagne had already, first thing, trickled down her hand.

"Copywriting, that does takes a nimble mind"—oh God, he was
British. Now it didn't matter what he looked like or what kind of horrible
person he was.

Bette wiped her hand furtively on her skirt. "You think so? I
definitely don't think so. I one hundred percent do it for the money."

Blake squinted in that way of British artists.

"What kind of art do you, um, do?" Bette asked. The woman at the
piano had finished a piece and the room was quiet.

"Photography, mostly. Bit of acrylic when commissioned."

Walter pressed his hands together, not quite wringing them. He was
such a soft, clever, genteel lady of a man; tenderness surged through
Bette. "Blake lost his mother some years ago. And Bette, you've also
experienced loss," he looked at her meaningfully, as though he wanted
her to pick up the thread. When she didn't, he seemed flustered. "Excuse
me, I need to check the nuts."

Bette wanted to ask Blake how he wound up in Birmingham, Alabama,
and how he'd lost his mother, but she knew the answer to both questions
could be summed up with the same answer—*life is weird*—and she
realized, knowing this, that she didn't much care for the details. There
was a time when she did care, and used questions to convey her interest.
Now she just waited as patiently as she could for things to be over.

Wandering into the TV room, she was startled to find a large boy.
He was staring down intently at the gaming device in his hands, but

 when he glanced up, Bette was alarmed by the magnitude of each of his features. His bottom lip looked as though it could crush her. His feet were like two toboggans. Bette edged out of the room, thankful for her petite children. The stress of having to keep such a person fed and clothed—that would be what sent her over the edge. Not everything else. And then, all at once, she felt that maybe she'd had it all backward, maybe if she had a giant child such as this one, he could flatten the rest of her worries into nothing. "Bye," she said weakly, and although his ears were enormous, he appeared not to hear her.

Walter's furniture and tableware were beautiful, heavy, old— everything in his house felt inherited, like it belonged to someone now dead. The table was covered in lace and shone in the slick brown and jewel tones of Southern fare—blood red tomato aspic, marigold eggs, the Ritz cracker-covered casserole, pork tenderloin, bourbon custard, pickled shrimp. Bette drained her glass and refilled it—coupes were elegant but held such a miserly amount—and then heaped her plate with a little of everything. She was surprised by the pride she felt when she saw how quickly her eggs and casserole disappeared, overheard several people say how good they were. She'd made them mostly while crying.

She sat on the end of the couch and perched her plate on her knees. She hated eating this way in public; hated eating in public in general. She set her champagne on the coffee table, which was too far away to be of any use. Blake sat on the piano bench opposite. Bette had an image of herself holding up her plate and doing like Sharon Stone in *Basic Instinct*, crossing and uncrossing her legs with languid extravagance. She stifled a giggle. The plate would really change the moment.

A couple asked if they could share the sofa.

"I'm Stephanie," the woman said. "How do you know Walter?"

Bette took her time chewing and swallowing. She would not be rushed for this person. "I think we met through a friend of my husband's.

A couple of years ago maybe."

Stephanie was the type who put food on the very end of the fork tines, mouse bites she'd learned from an overbearing mother. There was a whiff of ketones about her, the overall haunt of an old anorexia not fully shaken.

"Is he here? Your husband?"

Bette filled her fork, overfilled it. "No."

"This is Greg," she said, shifting to make him more visible. "Greg, this is—"

"Bette. Hi."

"Cool name," he said. "Bette, like Midler?"

"No, like Davis," she corrected. "But it's Bette, not Betty." The crease of puzzlement on their brows was satisfying.

Walter came over to refill glasses. "Oh good, I see you've met Greg and Stephanie. Greg's grandma died—last year, was it? She was a fine lady—Advent congregation, was it? And Stephanie—who have you lost, dear?"

"Um, both my grandfathers. And an aunt."

"Bless your heart," Walter said, moving to the next huddle. His steps were light as air; Bette had never seen him so happy.

Stephanie, seemingly from nowhere, was saying something about having lived in New York in her twenties. People who'd lived in New York in their twenties and people who'd gone to Harvard suffered under the same compulsion: to share these facts, no matter the context or the conversation. Bette, too, had lived in New York in her twenties, but she was the exception. She never talked about those years. Those years were a black stupid hole of nothing.

"... so tiny. I don't miss that. But the energy, the *culture*. But, you know. Greg doesn't even like going to Atlanta, so a bigger city was out of the question."

 Bette nodded politely, picturing this woman's setup, the meager thrills for which she'd brewed, in the dull years that had elapsed, such a pungent tincture of nostalgia: two or three roommates, the skim milk in the dingy refrigerator, the framed Klimt poster, the pastel-colored razors in the never dry shower. A Broadway show. A make-out session in Times Square. Then she stood, carried her plate and glass to the kitchen, and found Walter.

"I'm leaving now."

"Bored already?" He'd been talking to Blake and a bald guy.

"Sorry. It did seem to happen pretty quick."

"I was just fixing to play Bach's Toccata and Fugue in D minor. You'll miss Aunt Hebe's coconut cake."

Bette kissed his sweet, slightly stubbled cheek. "Next time, okay? Thank you for everything."

✵ ✵ ✵

Initially it was cloud talk, a kind of dare. George had been an infant.

"If we're going to the trouble and expense of finding a babysitter, then I deserve to leave the minute I get bored," she'd said, checking her lipstick in the passenger seat of the Yaris. Andrew was driving. "Technically, literally, my time is worth more than people who aren't paying sitters by the hour. I shouldn't have to pay money *and* suffer fools." She'd been wanting to test out "suffer fools" for a while, and was pleased with how it sounded.

"I mean, you can do what you want, I guess. But there's also something just called basic human decency. And if you did that, I'd have to leave with you, when I might not be ready to leave," Andrew said. "It's … selfish."

"Don't you think by now we have the same idea about what constitutes boring? I feel like half of our relationship, at least, is built on the foundation of finding the same things boring."

Andrew shrugged. "Yeah. I guess. But what if the person who's boring you is *also* paying a sitter? Then your time isn't worth more." He was already handsome and was getting more handsome with age. It's not that Bette wanted an ugly husband. She just wanted time to stop playing favorites.

"It doesn't matter," she said. "If I'm bored, I'm leaving. We're leaving. I've lost so much of my life to boring people already," she sighed, chewing a hangnail. She tried biting it off. They were passing her favorite sign, YESTERDAY'S SERVICE ... TODAY'S TECHNOLOGY, which featured large-scale graphics of an old-fashioned telephone and a computer from the 1980s. "You know, it's not even boredom, all the time. Sometimes it's impatience. Like when you have to listen to the postal worker ask if there's liquid, lithium, or perfume in your package, every single time. It's like, just get to the good part. But then there's no good part."

From that night on, they started leaving parties. They became The Leavers. It was a rare party they stayed at to its natural conclusion. They'd go to a bar, or to get ice cream, or if the spirit moved them, to the 24-hour Walgreens on Crestlake Boulevard. They'd buy candy and cotton balls, some dish soap if it was on sale. They felt bound by no man, no earthly etiquette.

But now, Bette left parties alone, when she went to them, which wasn't so very often. Sometimes she felt she missed leaving with Andrew more, even, than she missed being with Andrew.

✿　✿　✿

Alone now, she went to the Parkview and ordered a Coke. She didn't like drinking once there was a bunch of food in her stomach. Drinking was for getting buzzed, which happened most efficiently before dinner. Andrew could drink and drink, but it was easy for her to stop, to be done.

98    She was aware of herself as a forty-two-year-old woman drinking Coke alone at a bar. It felt in some ways like the most dangerous thing to be. Everyone around her looked stylishly unwashed. How could there be, she wondered, so many couples in one room, and not the slightest whiff of sexual tension. Was sexual tension passé? She worried, not quite like a mother, about this generation. Like an aunt, maybe, someone a little less invested. When she and her friends were twenty-somethings, they were trying so hard—to succeed, to be liked, to be loved, to be beautiful. They hugged easily, cried over a bit of bad luck. These girls seemed impenetrable, like they'd leveled up from apathy and achieved total cosmic armor. The wrung-out boys they were with, men, whatever—they never had to fight for a minute of porn in their lives. All of it, everything, it was right there, all the time. It was like, the more accessible the mysteries of the world were, the more dead-eyed its inhabitants.

Bette sucked the last of her Coke through the straw. She missed not knowing things. She missed sitting in rooms filled with people who couldn't remember the actor's name, their collective forgetting an intoxicating perfume, drawing them in closer, survivors of a neural shipwreck, castaways on If Only We Knew island. All of that was gone now, replaced by constant zippy, ugly, fluorescent answers.

"Another Coke?" the shaggy bartender asked.

"No, I'm good," she said. She put a five on the bar, too much for one Coke plus tip, but she didn't feel like talking to him again.

✻   ✻   ✻

The babysitter insisted that nobody'd had any candy, but when Bette bent close to George's sleeping, open mouth, she could smell Skittles under the toothpaste. *Nose of a bloodhound, this one,* Andrew used to say proudly around their friends. *Could smell a fart in Russia.*

Stupid babysitter, she thought, as she gently moved George's smushy body closer to the wall and got into his little bed. She pressed her face against his face, feeling so keenly how very hers he was. It was impossible for her to feel sleepy around her children; they were like epinephrine to her bloodstream. George drew from her body as though he were still inside it, each deep breath taking something from her. She shifted onto her back. The glow-in-the-dark constellation stickers on the ceiling had lost their glow; in the light from the hallway they looked yellowed and dingy. Andrew had stood on the bed last year and held George up as he peeled off each sticker and stuck it up there, not a single planet in the right place. She'd wanted to rearrange them.

*He'll learn the galaxy wrong,* she'd said. *He put Earth the farthest from the sun.*

Whenever she looked back on their exchanges at night, softened by alcohol, they had a certain poetry to them, a foreboding, even. For this reason, she didn't like thinking about Andrew at night. She no longer liked poems or poetry or anything that obfuscated truths or changed according to context. Right after Andrew left, she gave her forty-seven volumes of poetry to the local library, which felt like the most causal, normal response. All her life she'd avoided absolutes and now she loved them, longed for them, grids and graphs to live her life in, to raise her children in. She hated everyone's mealy-mouthed odes to freedom. Freedom and happiness had nothing to do with one another. Freedom was a pedophile and a phony. Poetry was a lie.

The nightly depression was starting.

She got out of George's bed and went across the hall to Liesl's room. Her sound machine whirred confidently, like a man snoring. It was the only thing she'd wanted for her last birthday, and Bette never understood how she could sleep through it, much less find it soothing. The fourth *Harry Potter,* the one she read over and over, was splayed spine-up on the bedspread next to her. Bette wanted to get in bed with her, too, but she didn't feel welcome, the almost-teen air like something spiky, an invisible warning. She leaned down and kissed her daughter lightly on the cheek, still smooth as a baby's. She kissed the hand that lay, but for the ragged cuticles, like the hand of a fainted, painted duchess. She looked at the photo of the four of them, Bette, Andrew, Liesl, and George, in front of a lighthouse in South Carolina, that sat in its Walgreens frame on the bedside table, and felt the burn of something old, an old feeling, one that predated her, a feeling of missing what was still very much there, still very much hers.

✻   ✻   ✻

Bette awoke before dawn from an athletic sleep. In the morning her hopes were highest. That was the circadian rhythm of her outlook: high hopes in the morning, waning toward afternoon, bottoming out with the sun. Nights were full-fledged gloom events.

A single bird called plaintively. Fran the cat was curled at the foot of the bed. She only slept on the bed when nobody was looking. Bette softly *tspst*'d for her—who decided on that sound for cats, she wondered, always a little self-conscious around animals in a way she wasn't with children—and Fran looked up like she'd been knifed and bounded away. *How dare you desire me.*

Light pressed itself against the darkness, bruising it. She touched the unmarred pillow next to her, slanted her body into the emptiness where Andrew's body used to be, still and warm as a sunbaked rock. It was cold there now. Bette marveled, just for a second, at the different temperatures one bed could hold. The bed, a mere queen, felt enormous, as though she could stretch and stretch and never find the edges of it. She thought of her children, of every corner of her life, and as if on cue, the bewilderment swelled up and over like a creek after rain. Probably, she thought, it had always been gurgling there, but Andrew had dammed it. Now he was gone and there was nothing between her and overflow, and drowning. She closed her eyes and tried to organize her thoughts—the kids were downstairs, safe and sound. It was Sunday. She'd promised to help Liesl with a project that required poster board. Everyone's closets and drawers were too full, which always made Bette uneasy. There was a water bill she'd meant to dispute last week. The living room rug was stained where George had dripped something. Her left eyebrow ached. Her children were individuals with their own thoughts and secrets and prejudices; they might be murderous or negligent one day. Time was ravaging her face and body. CIA operatives were torturing people in distant lands. She had four overdue library books, two of which she couldn't find. She was going to visit Andrew for the first time since he'd been at Apple Hill.

Everything felt equally impossible. She'd lost her sense of scale.

She heard feet, George's, shuffling up the stairs. Liesl was not a shuffler.

"Mama," his voice called sleepily through the door.

"Come in, my sweet."

He padded to the bed and got in on Andrew's side. Bette spooned him lightly and matched her breath with his. She tried to let each breath cancel out a thought but it didn't work.

"My foot hurts," he said.

"Why?"

"I stepped on a Lego."

Bette reached down and rubbed his foot.

"The other one."

She rubbed his other foot. "Is that better?"

"No."

Liesl appeared in the doorway, her hair a child's scribble-scrabble

**102**   drawing of hair.

"Get in," Bette said.

She climbed in on Bette's side. Now Bette was in the middle, her head wedged between the two sets of pillows. She thought about the people who insisted on sleeping with their kids every night—"co-sleeping," as though sleep required more than one person's participation—and hated them all instantly, and felt refreshed by her hatred, better prepared for the day. You can't just go sticking "co-" in front of any old word, she thought. What could be more solitary, more lonely, more autonomous than sleep?

"Are you going to see Daddy today?" Liesl asked. She would never say "Daddy" in front of her friends, only "Dad."

"Yes," Bette said.

"I want to come!" George twisted around, kicking her in the shins.

"No," Bette said. "Not this time. Next time, maybe."

"When is he coming back?" Liesl asked.

"I don't know."

"Can we watch TV?"

"Yes."

Nobody moved. The room was streaked with light. Bette's body was always a little sore and she'd generally assumed it was because she was forty-two and constantly trying to change its shape, lift heavy things, move her legs faster than they wanted to go. But now, flanked by two sets of spindly, furry limbs, it occurred to her that the soreness was the result of being something much heavier than a person—she was, against her wishes, a trudging fortress, buckling from the answers and assurances and ingots of comfort that were now part of her flesh. Being a mother meant you had to know everything twice. When George and Liesl came to her, they came in a perpetual state of seeking. Schedules, snacks, square roots, state capitals, what happens when you die. Whatever she said, they believed, unquestioningly. How on earth did that happen? Bette was the single greatest liar she knew.



✵   ✵   ✵

Apple Hill was in Florence, about two hours from Birmingham. The driveway was inconspicuous, with a mailbox that looked like the mailbox of an ordinary house. Bette drove slowly, seat warmer on despite the mild weather, the minivan bearing her forward like a living thing. The heat beneath her made her feel less alone.

She parked in the lot marked "Visitors and Volunteers." Trees were everywhere; she'd never seen such a display of trees, outside of an actual forest. Magnolias? Oaks? She had no idea. There were people who knew birds and trees and flowers, and people who didn't and never would.

In the lighted visor mirror, her skin looked waxy. She folded it up and then back down again. Still waxy. She pulled a tissue from the box she kept in the huge console between the driver and passenger seats and daubed her face, smoothed her eyebrows, put on lip balm. It had been six weeks and three days since she'd last seen Andrew, since he'd told her that he didn't want to leave but couldn't stay.

Why did she cry when kids on TV shows were abused, but not when her husband told her that the fact of his abuse as a child was making his life as an adult a living hell? Kids who were abused grew up, if they did at all, to become adults who had been abused. No amount of years could change the abuse. Yes, of course, she knew this. She would never expect the fake-abused fake-child on the TV show to "grow out of" their abuse. She'd tried picturing Andrew as not only a child but as a child on TV, to see if it would make the tears come, if it would help her respond to adult-Andrew with the compassion he deserved.

It didn't work. She'd told him to get out, to get in his stupid Yaris and just go. *I'll tell the kids you left us because—what? Someone did something terrible to you. And now you're doing something terrible to them, abandoning them. Can't you just—*

Get over it, she almost said, but didn't. She didn't tell the kids about the terribles, either. She told them their father needed some time away, a special kind of treatment, so that he could feel happier.

*Is Dad going to a nuthouse?* Liesl had asked.

*Corbin's allergic to nuts,* George had said. *If he eats one, he'll die. Is Daddy going to die?*

*Not the nuts you eat, dummy. Nuts as in* crazy.

Bette had stood at the kitchen island, calm in her stained shirt, in the midst of what had turned out to be, she hated to notice, an excellent hair day. All day at work she'd been lavished with compliments.

*Daddy is not crazy, and he is not in a nuthouse. He's in a quiet place where people go when they need some time to think. He's there because he loves us and wants to be the best person he can be. For us. We'll get to visit, and he'll get to visit, and before we know it, he'll be home.*

It had been six weeks, and there had been no visits. He talked to the kids by phone once a week.

Bette walked toward the building, which looked like a comfortable manor from the front and a 1950s community center from everywhere else. Bette kept expecting someone to ask her who she was and what she was doing, but there was no one, no security, no locked doors, even. She walked in and was greeted warmly by a man at the front desk. There was a fireplace, couches and rugs, a big bookshelf filled with books. Lamps.

"Just sign in. I'll let him know you're here."

A woman with a corgi came in.

"How'd it go today, Susan?"

"Great. She did such a great job."

"Glad to hear it." He smiled at Bette. "Room 223. Down the hall, make a right, and there's an elevator. Or there are stairs just off the elevator, if you wish." He enunciated like an elementary school teacher.

The corridor beyond the cozy front room was tiled and had just been mopped. She stepped around the *Cuidado* cone. She took the stairwell to the second floor and found Andrew's door open. He was propped on the bed, reading, feet bare and relaxed. The room looked like a college dorm, plain but not sterile. A daffodil drooped in a blue plastic cup on the bedside table.

"Well, hi," he said, getting up.

"Hi."

They stood facing each other. They'd been in a relationship more than half their lives. Bette used to say that she could have filled a rain barrel with all the tears she'd cried over Andrew in her late teens and early twenties. Her body felt perfectly arid.

"You look good," she offered. He'd grown a light beard.

"Thanks. I feel good," he said. "Do you want to sit down?" He indicated the desk chair.

"Sure." She sat. He resumed his position in the bed. The book, facedown, was titled *The Body Keeps the Score.*

"So," she said. She wanted to scream. She didn't like being a visitor, not here, not in museums, not in hospitals. She only liked being home. "Is it—working?"

Andrew chuckled. "I guess. I think so. It's good to be here."

"As opposed to with your family?" Bette focused on controlling her voice. She could be the calmest angriest person anyone had ever known.

He gazed at her with a gaze that felt practiced. Maybe he was in, Bette thought, Gazing Therapy.

"I've never asked you for anything. And I'm not asking you for this. This is necessary for me. You can understand or not understand, but to not understand is a total rejection of me and everything I've been through."

"But it's like—Andrew." She suddenly wished herself back at the funeral party. *My husband, it's my husband who died*, she imagined saying to the group, Blake and Walter and the boring New York lady. There is more than one way, she thought now, to be dead. "It's not just me. You have kids now. You have responsibilities. And what does that mean, 'you've never asked me for anything'? Of course you have. We're married. Marriage is the world's most enormous Ask."

"The way I see it," he said, folding his hands, "it's my settlement money paying for this. It's my leave of absence from work. It's my right to take care of myself."

"That money could have been Liesl's college tuition. An emergency fund for God-knows-what. Don't you think you're being even a tiny bit selfish?" The daffodil was infuriating her. So smug.

Andrew sighed. "This is why I kind of hoped you wouldn't visit. We're not getting anywhere. You know how much I love the kids, or you should know. This is a drop in the bucket, and will be so much better for them in the long run."

Bette stood up. She couldn't bear his voice sitting down for another second. "Okay, fine, then—what about me? Forget the kids for a minute. What about me?"

"When is it not about you? It has always been about you. It's about you right now, no matter how many times you bring up the kids. It's about you even when it's actually about *me*. This time it's about me."

Bette looked at him, at the bed. For a moment she'd thought maybe they'd wind up in it together. She could still imagine touching him, but she couldn't imagine him touching her, or wanting to. She glanced at the open doorway, wondering if any other couple had ever had an exchange like this—I deserve, no I deserve—in this room.

"Okay, well, I'm gonna go," she said. She felt the way she used to feel as a kid on Easter, white patent shoes too tight, stomach sugary and hollow, depressed. She still didn't know what *alleluia* meant.

"Bye, Bette. I hope you can find some way to understand. For all our sakes."

✿   ✿   ✿

She called her best friend Eleanor before she even exited the parking area. She didn't feel like crying; she felt like yelling. She was lucky, she knew, to have in her life women she cried to and women she yelled to.

"Can you please just move here? It's so much cheaper than Portland," she followed the winding driveway back to the road, going faster than she should have.

Eleanor's voice, loud and scornful, came through on Bluetooth. "You are the only person I'd ever move to Alabama for, and there's no way in hell I'm moving to Alabama."

"Listen," Bette said, "you could have an actual garden. Like a big one. There's a house on my block with the best yard you've ever seen. And it's probably a quarter of what you're paying for your apartment."

"Well, I mean, it ought to be. It's *Alabama*," Eleanor jeered.

For a few seconds it was completely quiet.

"It's going to be okay," Eleanor said. "It's not going to be like this forever. And if you guys can't work it out, then truly, none of us can."

"I just don't understand how, for so many years, he was fine."

"Why does it matter? People change in all kinds of ways. Be glad it's this and not a mistress or a steampunk sleeve tattoo."

"But," Bette was desperate for Eleanor to be mad with her, "this isn't like he changed. It's like he *decided*."

"Oh, Jesus, Bette," Eleanor said, "no one *wants* to deal with what he's dealing with. It's not like he suddenly left you to become a painter in Paris."

 "UGH why are you defending him?" Andrew didn't make her cry, Bette thought, but Eleanor might.

Eleanor's voice downshifted. "Men are assholes. I'm sorry that you're straight and I'm straight. And I know this situation completely sucks. But it's going, I promise, to be okay."

They said their goodbyes and Bette turned off her GPS and drove around for another hour, never fully getting lost, until it was close to the time she'd promised the babysitter she'd be home. She pulled into her driveway the same person she'd been when she left, having solved nothing.

✿   ✿   ✿

Parenting Liesl and George by herself wasn't hard, exactly. If anything, it felt easier to govern under one monolithic energy, her own, versus the dots and dashes of administrating with Andrew. He was lenient where she was firm (the inverse was not true; Bette was always firm), cutting-the-crusts-off permissive, liberal about what passed for a made bed. The kids would bounce between their expectations like pinballs, ever ready to make their case or switch their loyalties.

There was no switching, now. There was only one jurisdiction. Peace, for the most part, reigned.

But at night, Bette felt Andrew's absence like an abscess, like a lost tooth, a physical thing that she could run her tongue over and be reminded of. How adults always responded to kids who complained "it hurts when I do *this*"—*well, then, stop doing that*—except that she *couldn't* stop. Memory was not like moving your arm a certain way. Memory happened whether you wanted it to or not. Andrew was still everywhere in a complete and living way; his pillow still smelled like his head had just been on it.

To clarify: she wasn't sad. The smell of his head made her angry.

She folded George's small T-shirts and Liesl's many pairs of jeans while meal-planning in her head and paying bills from her phone, and her rage simmered at a low boil like an old family recipe. At work, she smiled and met deadlines and ran meetings and had leftovers at her desk while everyone else on her team went to Olive Garden for a Never-Ending-Pasta-Bowl™ eating competition. In the evenings, she emptied folders and lunchboxes and puzzled over homework and read with George in his bed and sat cross-legged with Liesl on hers, gently prodding about the day. Often she fell asleep before ten after reading the same page she'd re-read the night before and then would awaken in the dead of night, bloated with the Feeling, the dread-ennui-terror-blindness, helpless until her alarm went off at six.

✿   ✿   ✿

It wasn't that Bette hadn't known about Andrew's past; she'd known since their third or fourth date. Part of what had drawn her to him was his pluck; he seemed like the most okay person in the world, funny and quick-witted and wise and, though she'd always loathed the term, a good sport. From him she learned that trauma could be survived and even, in the hands of the lucky few, inculcated with mutant powers, transmogrified into a wellspring of empathy and humor. Also, he believed in God, in the best, cynical sort of way, and so she started believing in God, too.

A lot, maybe, for a young relationship to bear—God and trauma and youth itself—but bear it, it did. They broke up and made up a few times, and then they made up forever by getting married.

Many ordinary and extraordinary things happened, as is the case in any relationship with a vocabulary, with a stenographer. Bette assumed the role, inventorying with photo albums and diaries and her pages-long birthday letters to Andrew and the children, recounting the highs and

**110**  lows of the year gone by. It was a way to mark time, but it was also, she knew, a way to lay the past down, commemorate it so that she could move on. A funeral party for the mere passage of time and whatever incidents—lost teeth, summer vacations, acquired skills—time happened to get snagged on.

*I don't have much patience for the past,* Bette had said, late one night, months ago, when Andrew had first told her that he was struggling, that he needed space.

*Okay, that's fine, but can you at least have patience for me?* He was leaning against the refrigerator, sad and handsome.

Bette hesitated, unsure of how to answer. History, she thought, will remember me as the most heartless wife in the world.

*I can try.*

❃   ❃   ❃

*Why now,* she'd moaned to Eleanor on the phone a few days later, still reeling, still seething. She and Andrew had not spoken much.

*Probably because he has children of a certain age. Who knows? It wouldn't be trauma if it were neat and orderly and checked with your schedule first.*

*Of course, of course, of course,* Bette had said. She didn't feel like a monster but she knew she ought to have. Why didn't she feel like a monster? At night, awake, alone, everything around her foreign and mean—that was, maybe, the monstering. That was her punishment for needing her husband to—no, you're not allowed to say it, not even inwardly—*get over it.*

*Do you ever just get tired of that word, "trauma,"* Bette asked Eleanor during that same phone call.

*No. But I'm sure I would if I were you.*

*I wonder which of us will die first.*

*Who? You and me? Or you and Andrew? The men always die first,* **111** Eleanor said.

Bette tried to laugh. *Put it on my headstone: I'm a nightmare to be married to but a very good wife.*

*You're* so *good. I'd marry you in a second. And bury you wearing Valentino. But you'd have to move here first, I don't think girls can marry each other in Alabama yet.*

*It hurts my feelings when you make fun of Alabama all the time.*

*I love you, my little weirdo. Go make your husband a sandwich or something.*

Bette did make Andrew a sandwich, a great one. Sandwiches were how she said I love you and how she said I'm sorry. Sandwiches did emotional labor where she fell short. And as they approached what was more and more undeniable as middle age—the minivan, the rolls of antacid in the dishcloth drawer—Bette found that she was frequently falling short, or that the tolls had increased. It wasn't that he needed her; in fact, it was just the opposite. If he'd needed her she would have been okay. He seemed to need everyone and everything else: therapy, therapies, support groups, group chats, matinees ("me time"), long and sudden naps.

She made him sandwiches through all of it. He still had the best personality of anyone she knew. But he didn't feel like a husband anymore. He felt like a troubled brother.

✲ ✲ ✲

She forced herself to do the math and discovered that she'd spent over a thousand dollars on babysitters in the past two months. She stared at the number, afraid for a few seconds that if she had any kind of reaction at all, it would come out as the type of long, shrieking howl that mothers get arrested for. When she felt the danger pass, she texted a sitter.

"Why can't I come see Daddy?" George pouted, upside-down on the couch, bare feet kicking and dirty.

"Well," Bette made her voice casual and patient, "kids aren't really allowed, where Daddy is," she said. On one hand, she couldn't imagine children at Apple Hill. On the other hand, it was so easy to lie.

"Liesl's going to spend the day at Maggie's, so you'll get Melissa all to yourself," she said. Melissa was George's favorite sitter, the one who was available the least.

"Yay! Can we go to the park?"

"Yes. You can go to the park, you can get ice cream. I saw the truck the other day."

"Best day EVER," George said, folding himself off the couch.

"Best day ever," Bette repeated.

In the minivan, she tried to clear her head. She'd essentially been paying babysitters so that she could clear her head. The feeling was that of wanting to *do* something, or more accurately, wanting to *have to* do something, so that maybe, for a couple of hours, she could stop feeling everything. She thought about going to The Container Store and buying containers, things that she could put other things into, which seemed like as good a place as any to start. But the idea of all those rows of overpriced plastic made her feel anxious, and she knew she'd leave depressed over how much money she'd spent and how utterly inadequate her organizational skills were. She'd rather throw everything away than keep it forever in plastic bins. In an instant, she realized that there was, really, no difference between the two, that sheathing something in plastic and putting it on a high shelf was just a creative way of throwing it out, of not dealing with it. Wouldn't the better goal be whatever the opposite of The Container Store was?

She'd driven to McDonald's almost without realizing it. She ordered

large French fries and a Coke. While she waited at the drive-thru window
she rummaged around in the console until she found the beat-up *OK
Computer* disc that skipped on tracks two and three. Why should she
give up basic joys, just because her life felt highly improbable? If Nero
fiddled while Rome burned, surely she could drive around eating French
fries and listening to Radiohead for a single afternoon while her husband
vigorously ministered to his psyche.

The despair would come back, she knew. But it was releasing her now,
to the simple but startling reminder that nothing—not this curiously
uplifted feeling, not Andrew at Apple Hill—lasted forever. So what if
he needed, or even wanted to be there for a while. So what if her life
felt tossed. She got on the highway toward Florence, wanting to share
her good news but not sure she'd actually drive all the way there. The
only permanence was death, from which she felt—window down, hot
salt on her fingers, Thom Yorke's comforting, ridiculous warble filling
her ears like the sea—very, very far. &<



· · · · · · · · · · · · · · · · · · · · · · · · · · · · · · · · · · · · · · · · · · · · · · · · · · · · · · · · · · · · · · · · · · · ·

*Kristen Iskandrian is the author of the novel* Motherest *(Twelve). Her story "Good With Boys," which
appeared in Issue No. 109, was included in* Best American Short Stories 2018. *She lives in Birmingham,
Alabama, and is co-owner of Thank You Books, a new independent bookstore.*

# VISIBILITY

EMMA WINSOR WOOD

When I lived in California, every tree was outlined in black, the poet says.

Downshifting down the narrow winding road, I notice a landscape of spiderwebs on the actual landscape, glowing spectral, wet, in the fog.

I used to wonder what distinguished "mist" from "fog"; now I know it's a question of visibility.

I am invisible here, in the fog.

My husband, C., is writing about "becoming-secret." He doesn't know exactly what that means, but hopes to propose a way of being outside

capitalism, now that "former modes of resistance have been subsumed into it."

After the reading, the poet calls the man she's seeing a "friend." I notice she wears a maroon band on her left hand, ring finger. She's childless, post-

menopausal. Did you say you have kids? she asks.

I reply as if I don't want them, but sometimes

I place a hand on my stomach and imagine something growing inside. A secret.

Without contacts, I can't see farther than ten feet. (That's fog.) With, I can see what looks like lavender purpling a neighboring slope. (That's mist.) We live in a small valley surrounded

by trees. Behind them, more trees.



*Emma Winsor Wood is editor in chief of* Stone Soup Magazine *and with C. Dylan Bassett translated* A Failed Performance: Short Plays and Scenes by Daniil Kharms *(Plays Inverse). She lives in Santa Cruz, California.*

# COMMUNITY PLOT

## BRYAN WASHINGTON

I'd started tending the ex's plot. The lettuce and the garlic and the turnips. It wasn't my idea, the apartment complex had a community garden, and of course I'd seen you out there but we didn't have shit to say to each other.

We met on the stairs after my guy left, and it was another few weeks before we spoke. I'd seen you around, though. Sometimes I'd catch you staring. Our eyes met, and you'd look away. You were an old man, living alone, always in the same greasy cardigan and the same burnt brown shoes, which was everything I never wanted to be, or so I thought, at least back then, and one day I told the ex all of that and he just gave me this look.

But then—the split.

Which left me solo.

Afterward, you only ever saw me in sweatpants, dumping six-packs of Karbach in the dumpster at the end of the week.

By then, everyone else's vegetables were jumping into bloom. I watched Isabella and Jiao and the other neighbors prune their soil indiscriminately. But all of my shit started dying, and I was never entirely sure what was wrong, because I'd never seen the ex break a sweat over the garden, which he'd maintained silently. Meticulously. Whatever he'd done seemed to work without a hitch.



Houston keeps a tropical climate. A boon for the earthier strains. In some ways, my fucking everything up was as remarkable as anything else.

One afternoon, I'd poured the last of like five water bottles over the spinach when you stopped me.

Kid, you said, that's not the way. You're gonna drown them.

Hasn't happened yet, I said.

That's a sign. It's the roots talking. You've gotta listen to them.

I'm good, thanks.

And then you nodded, like, All right, you little bitch.

You hobbled back to your own patch of green, with the mustard and the collards. They pulsed, blooming over everything else. Casting these big-ass shadows across the lot.

A few weeks later, everything was fucking dead.

Jiao and his kid watched me size up the remains. The soil cracked under our Vans.

Damn, he said. RIP.

Bullshit. They'll come back.

No doubt, said Jiao. We just might not be here to see it.

Then he and his kid crossed themselves, sending two fingers skyward.

I didn't have time to stage an agricultural revival. I was still working downtown. Still had the temp thing at the ex's office on Elgin and San Jacinto. We'd pass each other on the staircase and I'd think: I used to fuck you, you'd bend me entirely over a chair—once, twice, three times a day, even, I'd let you finish wherever you wanted, wherever you asked, at any time of day.

But what I actually said was, Hi.

And then the ex said, Hey.

And that would be that. We went right back to our new lives.

118 Then one day I came home to a crowd standing over my garden graveyard. Legit concern creased their brows. They were literally thinking aloud. What could've gone wrong? Everything'd been fine a few months ago. The owner had clearly fallen off, they needed their space revoked, it was an embarrassment to the community.

I watched everyone through my shitty little window.

And then I saw you, stooped over the railing.

I waited to see if you'd join in the fun, but you didn't even look up. You just tended your own shit and turned your back and walked away.

That weekend, I was waiting for a hookup to roll through when you knocked on my door. I answered in some boxers.

I said, You know where I live.

You just rolled your eyes. We were the only two black guys in the complex. Everyone knew where we lived.

These books sat under your arm. Their covers featured avocados and tomatoes strung together with looping vines. On one, a white woman perched over this granite counter, hidden under what looked like a discount sombrero.

Read the Kennedy first, you said. It'll bring your garlic back.

No shit, I said.

Correct, you said. The onions, too. Once the humidity's dropped, they'll recover.

I took the books from you, not really looking at their covers. We slumped in the doorway, kicking sideways at the carpet.

So, I said, and that's when you shouldered past me, and I'm not the smallest guy in Texas but you moved pretty quickly for an old fucking man.

You scoped out the walls of my apartment. Not that there was much to see. I had this PS4. A busted coffee table. A deck of torn playing cards. Miyazaki DVDs scratched beyond recognition. And for reasons I still

can't explain, I didn't do shit to stop you: I just watched you wander   
from room to room, wiping your fingers at all of the dust.

You'd grunt, from time to time, tapping and rubbing at the counter.

No books, you said.

Are you a goddamn librarian?

I'm a human being, you said. Open your brain.

I *work*, I said, but you weren't listening, already drifting again,
whistling now.

After a lap around the living room, you picked at a quilt on the sofa.
My grandmother, a devout homophobe, had knit the thing decades
back. I'd made a habit of fucking on it regularly, wrapping it around
my shoulders afterwards, and you sat yourself across from the thing,
crossing your legs at the heel.

Not much here, you said.

You're in a stranger's home, I said.

Well, you said, and then you let your gaze linger, sloping casually
to my legs.

It was pretty late now. My hookup still hadn't knocked. You extended
a finger, grazing my knee, and when I looked up, you'd raised an eyebrow.
If I hadn't done anything, hadn't fucking responded to your touch,
it's worth wondering what would've happened. How all this would've
turned out.

But I set a hand on your shoulder—and that was it.

You grabbed the backs of my knees, setting my ass on your khakis.
When I didn't give, you tugged harder, until I sort of collapsed on your
shoulders. With your toes on the carpet, you started pushing me out of
my sweats, before you, slowly, inched my back on the sofa.

Whoa, I said. Whoa whoa.

Do you need me to stop, you said.

You don't need to take it slower? Can you even do this?

120

Fuck you, kid.

I'm just saying.

I was fucking before you were born.

You look like you're right around the corner from the grave.

And you grimaced at that. But I relaxed a bit. It lightened the mood. Which meant that we were grinding, again, with my chest on yours, and your mouth on my ear and my lips on your neck, and I let you set the rhythm, until I decided not to do that anymore, and eventually, I grabbed our dicks with one hand, squeezing your shoulder with the other, and you groaned when I came, and I laughed when you came, and once you'd finished, gasping, I rolled off of your lap, waddling to the bathroom.

What we'd done, and how quickly we'd done it, didn't hit me until I'd finished washing up.

So I listened through the bathroom door. Thought about just letting you leave, because maybe you'd get the hint. You probably had kids. Grandchildren. A wife. The whole thing. It wouldn't be the first time. We'd pretend this shit never happened.

But then, from the living room, you said, It'll come back.

What, I yelled.

Your garlic. Once the cold spell's over, it'll come back.

That's really what you want to talk about right now?

It's what I knocked on your door for, kid.

Stop calling me that.

It's what you are.

I'm not a child.

Wait until you're my age. You'll wish someone called you kid.

Then the two of us sat silent on both sides of the door.

Well, I said. Thanks for nothing.

Look, you said. Kid. Guy. Whatever. Your plot looks like shit. It's

fucking up the garden. No one else will tell you this. Young guy like    **121**
you, they probably think you'll jump on them.

Guess that makes you a good fucking Samaritan, I said.

Let the cold front pass, you said, again, and that's when I finally
opened the bathroom door.

But you'd already made it down the hallway, shutting your own door
behind you. Leaving mine ajar. I thought you might turn around on your
way down, but that was just wishful thinking. You were already gone.

You weren't wrong about the garden, though.

My garlic had a big fucking resurgence. Tentatively, at first. But
now I had a list of instructions to conjure, an actual set of rules.

I switched up the supplements. Started measuring the water in
intervals. I trimmed the weeds surrounding my shit, made a point to
keep them away.

A month later, my plot looked like an entirely different thing.
Something living. Just barely, but still there.

Most mornings, I manicured everything while Isabella trimmed
her oregano.

You're the comeback kid, she said. Like Canelo.

You mean Creed.

I meant exactly what I said.

And every now and again, I'd catch you staring from afar.

I'd smile, and you'd nod, but I was the only one who looked surprised.
You never said a thing about it. But, then again, there was nothing else
for us to talk about.

So eventually I knocked on your door.

Took four minutes for you to answer.

You brought the books back, you said.

Duh, I said.

**122**  Presumably you've bought some of your own.

That's not what this is.

We were well into the evening. And here you were, just waking up, wiping at your eyes. I took a second to peek in your place, and it was immaculate, like something out of the airline catalogs. From the hallway, I could spot paintings of sprawling landscapes, and a phonograph by the kitchen. The apartment's wood was covered by this gigantic rug. Bookshelves sank into the walls.

Forget about the books, you said. Keep them. They're yours now.

You're bugging, I said.

I'm not. Call it a gift.

And by the way, you said, we're entering the fall. Everything of yours should be fine to eat soon. If that's something you were interested in.

I don't cook, I said.

That's why I'm bringing this up, you said. This is an offer.

You're offering to cook for me?

I have to say it a third time?

Like a date?

Don't overthink this, you said. The distance from your door to mine is thirty seconds at a brisk limp.

I looked at you in your cardigan and your khakis. Your hair wasn't all that gray. You'd taken care of your skin.

You wouldn't even fucking acknowledge me an hour ago.

And here we are, you said. Chatting. Acknowledging.

Look, I said, I don't know what you're getting after, but I'm—

I just said don't overthink it, kid.

You gonna let me finish?

No, you said. Look. Just invite me over.

What?

Right now, you said. Unless you've got something better to do.

I don't think that's a good idea.

You're sure?

We're standing in front of your place.

Come on, you said, shutting the door behind you, padding down the hallway in house slippers, opening my door, which I'd failed to lock.

And leave your shoes at the goddamn door, you said. No wonder it's so fucking dusty in here.

We took longer this time.

Started on one end of the hallway, ended up in my bedroom. You grabbed at my shoulders. I tore at your belt. You knelt down, spinning me, rimming me, and I let you do that, before you turned me over again, collapsing onto the mattress; and then I reached for your socks, raising your ankles, and when I stood over you, you shook your head, once, but with certainty—so I got on my back, and you straddled me, grinning. In the middle of it, you wheezed, coughing, and I asked if you needed a break, but you started up, again, a little too fast, with deeper strokes, until I was gasping, and then I came, and then you came, once and then once again.

I'd switched the sheets a few days back with this unopened pack from the ex. He'd always wanted to invest in nicer wares, but of course I wasn't used to spending money like that. Where I grew up, we had money for bills. That was it. Everything else went into a rainy day fund and it rained every day.

But now, you squeezed at my thigh. Your thumbs looped around my belly.

Are you having fun, I said.

I am, you said, still breathing a little too heavily. Your skin's so soft.

You're calling me fat, I said.

I'm calling you soft, you said.

But it's funny, you said, wiping the sweat from your ears. Usually

124 good fucks can cook well, too.

I think you just made that up.

Whatever, kid.

You think you can talk shit about me because we fucked?

I was only making an observation.

How long has it been for you, old man? A decade? Two decades.

Twenty-seven years, four months, and eleven days.

And then the two of us stopped talking. We looked up at the ceiling.

I don't need you to pity me, you said.

I don't.

Good.

But my offer stands, you said. The meal. If you want it.

I don't know, I said. It might be weird now.

Of course it would be weird.

We'd done a nice job of slowly separating our bodies on the mattress. You watched me from your corner, and I watched you from mine.

And you opened your mouth to say something, but nothing came out. I watched your chest rise and sink and rise and sink instead.

At some point, you unrolled yourself from the sheets. Wouldn't meet my face.

But as you grabbed at your clothes, I asked, a little abruptly, since it wouldn't have happened otherwise, if next week worked, around 6:30 in the evening.

You blinked. And then you nodded.

Let's say 7:00 instead.

Why, I said.

It's a lucky number, you said.

For the Chinese. You aren't Chinese.

If it's good enough for them, you said, but then you didn't finish your sentence, you just turned around and left.

Most nights, I just ordered out for dinner. The delivery guy from the Mediterranean spot down the way knew my first name. He'd actually almost made a move, once, and we'd grinded for a bit in my doorway, but then he got cold feet and it threw the whole fucking vibe off. Now, we only cheesed like we'd gotten away with some fucking heist, fumbling approximations of English between ums and ahs and hand gestures.

Sometimes, I invited Isabella and Jiao over. We'd lay everything out on the counter, the rice and the lamb shanks and the falafel and the soup. They'd ask how I was doing. I told them I was fine.

Liar, said Isabella.

You don't know that, I said.

I know you.

Calm down, said Jiao, snapping a plastic spoon.

I said, So what the hell does that make me?

Fucked, said Jiao.

Hey, said Isabella, your kid's listening.

We stirred the broth between us with a ladle. Jiao's son tumbled somersaults in the corner, singing to himself.

Maybe there's something, I said. Someone. A boy.

A boy? said Jiao. Or a man?

Shut up, I said.

Wasn't the last one younger than you?

By two months.

Two months is nothing, said Isabella.

All you do is chase grad students, said Jiao.

They have the stamina.

I thought we were talking about me, I said.

Calm down, said Isabella. So, your man-child.

He's a little older.

That's nice too, said Isabella. Older means stability. You can finally

126 move out of this dump.

You love this neighborhood, I said.

She loves it, said Jiao.

I love the price point, said Isabella. Let a tech prince offer to fly me out of it. I'd pack my shit tonight.

But your new dude, she said. That's good. This is good news, right?

Maybe, I said.

Jesus, said Jiao.

Jesus, said his kid, punching our knees under the table.

But that was the thing: you and I had concocted an inexact routine. A faulty equation.

Some days, we worked.

Some days, we did not.

Some days, you'd knock on my door with purpose, and books tucked in your armpits.

I learned that you were a florist. That you worked at the little Thai shop on Anita Street.

Oh shit, I said. The one with the red lettering on the door. By the noodle bar.

That's the one, you said.

I went there once. For an old boyfriend.

Your whiteboy.

He was white, yeah. But I've had other boyfriends.

I'm sure you have. And I bet they were white, too.

I bet it's none of your fucking business.

A florist though, I said. Hunh.

Don't sound so shocked.

I'm not shocked.

You sound like our fucking patrons. Everyone can appreciate a flower.

That's not what I meant.

That's exactly what you meant.

It's just different, I said.

You've only been alive for two minutes, you said. You wouldn't know different if it sat on your face.

You'd lecture me in the hallway about composting, or pimping Mother Nature's nutrients, until I'd reached the kitchen—now, I took off my shoes in the doorway—until we finally did it—fucked, I mean—standing up, or sitting down, or against the wall.

One day, we were catapulting across the apartment floor, and your back, suddenly, instantaneously, popped.

You rolled off of me immediately, groaning.

Fuck, I said, are you good?

I'm fine, you said. We'll keep going.

Is that a good idea?

Does it matter?

So you rolled over. I straddled you. We kept going, cracking your spine all the while.

By then, it was well past midnight. Afterward, you tried standing up from the tile, leaning on the counter, but you couldn't. I watched you dawdle for a moment as you tried to stand a second time, and then a third, but after your fourth stumble I walked you to the sofa by the bedroom.

Listen, I said. I don't mean to be a fucking asshole about this, but it's late.

I have a watch, you said.

Had you planned on staying the night?

The look you gave me could've melted ice.

That's what I thought, I said. But do you think you can make the walk to your place?

Do you think you've invented sex? you said.

I think you overexerted yourself.

Whatever, guy. I've been fucking longer than you've been—

You've already said that. Stay here.

I walked you to the bedroom, grabbing the same quilt you'd picked at on our first day. Wrapped it around your shoulders, with your bare knees poking beneath it. And you looked my way for a long moment before you asked, earnestly, I think, if I thought this was a good idea.

I'll be in your bed, you said.

And I'll be outside, I said. On the sofa.

Still. It's a bit intimate.

This is hardly a proposal.

Just a bit.

It's nothing. Don't wake me up when you leave. Just lock the door. Yell if anything else pops.

Then you said, Fuck you, and I shut the door behind me.

When I got up to piss a few hours later, I checked on you. You were snoring, open-mouthed, sprawled on the mattress. Cradling the quilt.

I'd never asked about your age, but I pegged you about a decade younger than my mother. You could've been one of her students. She would've talked about you at my dinner table. Or maybe she wouldn't have.

One day, apropos of nothing, in a car ride to the airport to pick up my father, my mom said that no man ever changes your life. That was just something we told ourselves to justify their fucking up our situation.

A body is a body is a body, she'd said, driving, squinting.

You didn't wake me up when you left.

I didn't knock to check in on your back.

After that night, you and I nodded whenever we saw each other. I'd ask about your patch of earth in the garden, and you'd ask after mine.

I went to work and came back and tended the plot.



Stopped cheesing at the ex.

The neighbors hovered when I tended my greens. They asked about the resurgence, and how it'd happened.

I chalked it all up to luck, and I never mentioned you, not once, and you could've called me out, you could've shamed me from the stairway.

Except you didn't.

Whenever I passed your apartment, I'd smell all sorts of craziness, chiles roasting and salmon browning and miso bubbling, shit I can only recognize now, years later, and sometimes, you'd eye me dragging some guy up to my place, and I swear you couldn't help shaking your head.

But you never said another word about it.

And then one day I was walking up to my apartment when the ex reached out. There was, I think, no rhyme or reason for this. But he did.

We always think we know how we'll react in these situations.

I'd told myself it wasn't happening, wouldn't happen, and it didn't, until he knocked on my door, and then it didn't even take four minutes, he had his hands in my pants, my tongue on his chest.

When I let him out, you were standing in the hallway, headed toward the garbage disposal.

You saw me, and then the ex.

You turned right back around.

The ex turned around to make a face of his own, and I shrugged right back at him, like, Who knows?

He smiled, as if we were the same.

I knocked on your door a few hours later.

You answered so quickly that I thought you'd been waiting for it. You stood in a sweater and some shorts. A violin droned from somewhere inside.

That smells nice, I said. Whatever you're making.

What do you want, kid.

The sun hadn't set yet. The sky was a bloody orange. I asked why you didn't grow your own cabbage. One of the books you'd loaned me praised the veggie for 232 pages.

You looked at me a long time before you said that I didn't get it.

I was the one who'd needed them.

You'd bought the books for *me*.

Sauté something for one of your whiteboys, you said, and then you slammed the door, right on my fucking nose.

At a play for Jiao's kid, we both sat in the front row.

So, I said, let's say I have this friend.

A friend that isn't you.

Yeah.

Fascinating. What does he look like.

White dude. Tall.

Skinny?

Sure.

Okay, said Jiao. A tall, skinny white boy. The exact opposite of you. But not you. Will this parable end before the kids make it onstage?

If you shut the fuck up.

Sorry, sorry.

Long story short, I said, let's say my friend's fucking around with this guy. Some dude. Someone he's not really into, but you know.

I know.

Right. But then my friend's ex walks in on them.

Like something out of a movie.

Right. And now they aren't talking.

The seats behind us filled with parents, shuffling their iPads and cameras. A father sitting beside us jostled his kid on his lap.

Is your friend in a relationship? said Jiao.

No.

Then why does he give a shit what this other motherfucker thinks?

Who knows. Let's say there's a connection.

Like a Wi-Fi thing?

Something closer to the earth.

The kids waddled onstage in rancher uniforms. We waved at Jiao's kid, who waddled out last, beaming.

If they have this connection, said Jiao, they should know what to do. They'll know how to respond.

You're a wealth of knowledge, I said. Remarkably unspecific.

You sound like my kid's mom. Look! There they go!

Jiao's kid wandered onstage, in the thick of a classful of cowboys. They twirled silver batons topped with horse heads, kicking spurs. We stood, recording with our phones, shouting bloody fucking murder.

So a few nights later, you answered the door, and I was holding a dish of burnt enchiladas.

It was half past six. Your eyes were red, still slumping in pajamas.

Sorry, I said. I can leave.

No, you said. Come in. Really. It's fine.

We sat at your dinner table, which was entirely too immaculate. You'd been in the middle of cooking congee—it'd simmered for hours— and we ate that instead.

Is this coconut? I asked.

Among other things, you said. Sweet potato. Ginger.

I didn't know they went together.

You've got years of not-knowing to look forward to.

A guy played piano on the stereo behind us. You asked if I knew about Billy Strayhorn, and when I said that I didn't, you flinched. But here's something about your place: there were photos everywhere.

132 Framed on the walls. Over the sink. Lining the whole of your hallway by the bedroom.

A younger you stood with another man.

Crouching together in front of a field.

Smiling in front of a house.

Throwing peace signs in line at an airport.

He was dark and grizzled. Grinning like a motherfucker.

That's Riley, you said, on your third glass of red.

Riley?

That's his name.

You told me that the two of you met in the service. That you'd lived in Okinawa and Seoul and Brussels. You'd been in Berlin when the wall came down, until you'd moved home to Oklahoma City, and then Fresno, and then Houston.

Now I think he's in South Carolina, you said.

That's where he lives?

It's where he's buried.

I wasn't invited to the funeral, you said.

And then we sat there for a while.

I thought the evening was over, but you stood up for more wine. You poured some for yourself, before you grabbed a glass for me.

It's hard for us, you said, laughing.

Us?

You know, you said, and you tugged at your skin, gesturing vaguely around the room.

I don't know, I said.

There you go again. You're young. You don't know shit.

Yeah. But things are changing.

Change doesn't always reach everyone, you said. Sometimes, you're gone before it gets to you.

Riley always said I wasn't up for the challenge, you said. I thought he was right about that. Thought I needed him. But it turned out he's the one who couldn't hang.

By this point, you were dozing off. Leaning halfway out of your chair, giggling to yourself. So I told you I should get going, and that's when you started mumbling—and despite everything that told me not to, I walked you to your sofa.

You held me a little too tightly but it didn't really matter. You inhaled, and I watched your shoulders drop just a little. But then I settled you onto the cushion, and you wouldn't let go, and I wondered what would happen next, what I'd do if you dragged me down with you.

But then you opened your palms. You patted my face.

Good luck, you said, smiling, shutting your eyes.

Good night, I said, standing.

And when you saw me the next morning, of course you didn't say shit! Didn't even blink.

Too bad, I told Isabella.

Too bad, she said.

Must've been the enchiladas, said Jiao.

He's too old for you anyways, said Isabella.

At this point, my plot had become a playground for children. Their eyes only widened when they poked at the greens. My vegetables had become caricatures of themselves. They were entirely too extravagant. White folks appeared from out of nowhere with excuses to take pictures.

I kept cooking the excess with Jiao and Isabella.

I fucked whoever whenever I could.

You and I kept passing without speaking.

One day during lunch, the ex sat on my desk with take-out, asking if we could talk.

It all felt like sleepwalking. Like a sham. Like I should've torn

134  everything out by their roots.

And then I was locking my door one evening when you stopped it with your boot.

We hadn't spoken in weeks. You looked, for the first time since I'd known you, refreshed. Clean-cut.

You handed me a book. Thick and bursting from the binding.

Another one? I said.

Shut up, you said. Listen.

I'm leaving town for a few days, you said. And I need you to hold on to this for me, but don't open it. All you're doing is keeping it safe.

You looked at the book in my hands, and I looked at you.

Can't you ask someone else? I said.

Sure. But I'm asking you.

And then you turned your back, headed down the hallway.

Where are you going? I yelled.

Charleston, you said.

But I'll be back in a couple of weeks, you said. You won't be keeping that one.

A few days later, you had a heart attack. There's no point in dressing it up.

Isabella was smoking by the apartment's entrance, waiting for me. She asked if I'd heard, did I already know, and before I could say, What, the EMTs passed us on the stairs.

They'd already carried you out. Already cleaned you up from the apartment.

Later, I found out what actually happened: that you were dying. You'd been sick for months and months. You knew what was coming, and when, and probably how.

But, that night, when I asked the EMTs, they asked how I knew you.

And the thing is, I wasn't family.

Or even a friend.

I was nothing.

So they didn't tell me shit.

One lady asked why the fuck I cared.

That weekend, Jiao knocked on my door, and two women were standing behind him. He shrugged with his hands in his pockets, a little embarrassed.

One of the women smiled at me. She called me by name.

We heard about you, said the other lady. We just wanted to say hello.

They were your sisters. They'd driven down from Oklahoma. The women were nearly identical, but both of them were older than you.

They stood in front of some boxes. The remnants from your apartment. The ex called out from my bed, and I shut the door behind me.

When Jiao and I offered to carry everything down, the sisters didn't protest. Mostly they laughed. But they were sad laughs, or half-laughs. Laughs that were hard won.

Once we'd finished packing, I asked them to wait a minute.

I came back down with the book you'd given me. I still hadn't opened it, but your sisters flipped through it wordlessly.

It was a collection of photos. Photos of you and Riley. In the park, and on the plane, and lazing around in each other's arms, and I bit my tongue as your sisters paused at page after fucking page.

When your sisters had finished, they handed it back to me.

I won't, I said.

Too late, said one sister.

You have to, said the other.

If he gave it to you, she said, then he wanted you to have it.

He always had too many friends, said the first.

I wasn't sure if she was joking or what. I opened my mouth, but

136 nothing came out. And they'd already packed your life away, so they waved to Jiao and me, and then they climbed in their little white U-Haul and hooked a left at the intersection on Dunlavy.

The only thing left was your garden.

Nobody volunteered to touch it. One week passed of no one paying it any mind, and then another one after that.

Every now and then, someone would ask about it, but that's all they did. Nobody actually lifted a hand.

I had no right to it myself. I wouldn't have known where to begin. So I waited for someone else to pick up the slack.

Only, the thing is, everything just kept fucking *growing*.

First it was the bok choy. Then, it was collards. You'd started planting a patch of garlic, near the end, and all it did was sprout from one corner to the next.

There was no explanation, really. But I watched it all bloom.

This life you put in the ground. Growing through, beyond, and because of you.

I told myself that when it began to wilt, that's when I'd start to care for it.

That's when I'd make the time.

But I wondered when it would come. ✄

*Bryan Washington is the author of the story collection* Lot *(Riverhead). He received the Ernest J. Gaines Award for Literary Excellence and was a National Book Foundation 5 Under 35 Honoree.*

*Beasts*, 2019, acrylic on panel, 48 × 48 inches
courtesy: the artist

*Es brennt*, 2018, acrylic on panel, 60 × 48 inches
courtesy: the artist

*Feral seer III*, 2019, acrylic on panel, 60 × 48 inches
courtesy: the artist

*Hand & heart*, 2018, acrylic on panel, 40 × 30 inches
courtesy: the artist

ANNE SIEMS

*Swan Arm*, 2019, acrylic on panel, 30 × 24 inches
courtesy: the artist

ANNE SIEMS

*Fox on Hill*, 2018, acrylic on panel, 48 × 36 inches
courtesy: the artist

ANNE SIEMS

*Lizard*, 2018, acrylic on panel, 30 × 24 inches
courtesy: the artist

ANNE SIEMS

*Right Angle Tears*, 2018, acrylic on panel, 30 × 24 inches
courtesy: the artist

# EVERYWHERE WE GO
# PEOPLE WANT TO KNOW

JENNIFER RICHTER

how he's doing and because we don't have
a new answer or two-second true answer
we can bear to admit we mostly don't go
anywhere mostly we've been watching
the cedar show all week across the street
three huge trees dangling orange men
total chainsaw circus we used to picnic
by any construction site we could find
crackers juice boxes his stuffed animals
propped up facing the scrape roar dump
and lurch of dust today a kindergarten
class comes to watch I hear them first
chanting over the machinery's racket
*WE ARE THE GECKOS   WE ARE THE GECKOS*
*MIGHTY MIGHTY GECKOS   MIGHTY MIGHTY*
*GECKOS* he used to love that picture book
gecko-hero licking dust off its own eyeball
I love their tiny voices shouting mighty
shouting you can talk yourself into being
brave just use your words your outside
voice I've started hearing everything
as a message in the lopped-off trunks
the neighbors' tree house is a little ark
snagged and dry above the water line
in bed each night we clutch each other

steady ourselves on the rocking deck
below us our sleepless son thrashes
like an animal we didn't dream we'd be
at sea this long didn't dream he might
always struggle to stay above the dark
dark waves my heart sinking my heart
racing I'll always be listening like prey
for sounds of what's coming a warning
a voice Noah was given years to prepare
and exact plans this number of cubits
equals your family will all be fine but
all this morning's headlines offer me is
"A Rule of Thumb: If You See a Tsunami
It's Too Late to Outrun It" the new siren
drills in our town a comfort let's practice
not panicking let's keep looking for signs
the new ones at low points on the coast
are blue cartoons an open-mouthed huge
wave and stick figure scrambling away
we used to chant good job at everything
he did without our help first he learned
to cry himself to sleep we used to follow
what the books said turns out that works
he's still really good at it and we're still
standing outside his door listening silently
crying some books call his pain a journey
he has to take alone but the chirping geckos
hand in hand on the sidewalk are counting
off by twos Noah did what the voice said
good job it said to save them pair them up

# ON WANTING TO BE ONE MORE TIME A SURVIVABLE VOID SPACE FOR MY SON

JENNIFER RICHTER

I used to cut dreams out of poems
used to cut out my 150 mg b.i.d.
once a year and think maybe now
my brain's blackout shade will rise
by itself maybe my son won't need
to know this about me but I was
dreaming obviously everyone said
yes they'd seen him yes he's really
depressed but I couldn't find my son
in the crowd the back of every head
was his then one man raised his arm
to point me down dream street but
stopped said wait you don't look
enough like him to be his mom
make a face you have in common
how would he answer how are you
when my son's doctor calls he calls
me mom says mom can you tell me
what medication you take because
there's a good chance your son will
respond to that nineteen years ago
he wasn't responding I'd said yes
to drugs hours earlier which maybe
was why his heart needed monitoring

when the doctor aimed a tiny wire at
my son's slick still-in-me head he said
keep breathing I remember back then
my son used to cry for one of three
reasons my body knew each answer
now he's crying but not hungry he's
tired but not sleeping never sleeping
scared but can't say why he's crying
happiest with the neighbor's old cat
that sits and stares like my son does
at our bunny hutch that's been empty
for ten months for so long I've been
holding my breath today for fifty-five
seconds I watched the wildfire blaze-
and-bunny video and started reaching
for the screen I'm that man panicking
that man thinking no one's watching
thinking how is this not a dream how
can I get him to sleep my son used to
sleep on me like a bunny on my belly
please if anyone out there is watching
deliver my son once more into light
this time I can catch him that first time
I couldn't wait to hear him cry

*Jennifer Richter's most recent book of poetry is* No Acute Distress *(Southern Illinois University Press/ Crab Orchard Series in Poetry). She is an assistant professor of Creative Writing and English at Oregon State University.*

# THE SHOWCASE COURT

MARK CHIUSANO

It wasn't every day you got an offer like the one the Tuesday bball crew was tendered.

They were middle height, middle aged, middling talent. They had come to the game late in life (except for Imtiaz, of course, who used to be marvelous). They showed up every Sunday morning to bang the hell out of each other and score a few points.

They didn't play with others. It wasn't that they were unfriendly or cruel. In the beginning, when Jordan first tentatively suggested they get some exercise instead of sitting around all day, they weren't really good enough to join others' five-on-five games or even tight three-on-threes. There was Imtiaz—still slim, and still pretty decent then, working out the kinks from a flashy CYO career decades before. Christopher—a window installation tech now married with two kids. Nathan—still a bartender who had always done his own thing, who came to the games tired and hungover and haggard. And Jordan of course, the glue of the four of them, who had just felt so thrilled to be let into their midst when they met, way back in middle school.

They were not especially impressive to look at, their benefactor admitted, particularly in those first games at the YMCA gym. The four of them guessed they hadn't noticed him up there in the rafters, always on the elliptical, or working the wheel of the hand bicycle, nursing a limp.

150 They hadn't noticed because they were so focused, in the beginning, on staying on their two feet and not breaking anything. And then, on getting better, week after week.

There was something earnest and life-affirming, said the benefactor, and hopeful and human, and potential and here-and-now, concerning their friendly combat. For reasons I can't go into, said the benefactor, I no longer play myself, I only watch and I can't get enough of the watching. But in my playing days, I made it most comfortable for myself to do so. Which as you might imagine meant a location in warm weather. It's yours whenever you want it, and if I have a moment I'll drop by and watch a game. Well we're not exactly professionals, Jordan joked, don't know how interesting we'll be. Oh no, said the benefactor with a strange smile, you're wrong there, I think there's something much more promising about amateur play, the clash, the fun, the distinctions, the rivalries, the gravitas and knowledge about what you're truly worth, and the possibility that you might be different than you thought you were, that you have the capacity for change, whether good or bad—that all goes out the window when your face is on a billboard in the NBA. I find that I can't watch anything but amateurs anymore.

It was Jordan who was doing the talking, Imtiaz still taking shots. Christopher was practicing dribbling with two balls, something he'd only recently mastered. Where exactly is the place you're speaking of? Jordan asked. When the benefactor told them, Jordan said, how can we ever repay you?

They flew down to Fort Lauderdale for a four-day weekend on a Thursday night. The benefactor had made clear that they could have the site for as long as was amenable, explained that he was sure they'd want to stay as long as possible, but they all had jobs and things keeping them home. They packed small and economical backpacks with the clothing they'd need, plus gym bags with different pairs of shoes and

an extra jersey in case there wasn't a washing machine. Of course, **151**
they would find that there was a washing machine. Both Jordan and
Imtiaz took balls.

Christopher rented a car when they landed, from points he'd accrued
during travels to window conferences. Nathan slept in the back, Imtiaz
looking patiently out the window. Jordan couldn't contain himself.

This is unreal, he said, as the everywhere scenery of the highway
passed by, the directional app on his cellphone tweaking Christopher's
steady driving hand from time to time. What a dream, he enthused.

It's awesome, Christopher said agreeably, patting down a jiggling
right leg. When I was in Vegas for Salesconference, there was a gym
that all the techs had access to…

…and he was off, Jordan not really paying attention though he
nodded often enough to pretend.

Imtiaz piped up from the back. Faux-innocent: Chris, but I thought
Salesconference was in Phoenix this year?

Oh nah nah, Chris began, beaming, you're thinking of our appliances
convention, that one was a doozy, I came back overloaded with gadgets…
he continued. Nathan popped open an eye. He grimaced. Jordan mouthed
to him, *your teammate.*

In the beginning they had switched teams after each game, trying
the few permutations, mixing it up. But for some strange reason, the
games that were both most competitive and most enjoyable were when
they kept the same rosters: solid Christopher and haggard Nathan, vs.
perfect Imtiaz and old Jordan. Yes, Imtiaz was best and Jordan worst.

Christopher droning: And that's why they decided to do the display
in San Diego, which, you know, would've been stellar, but I had to
monitor an installation in Minneapolis.

Christopher paused.

Oh? Imtiaz said.

So I had to miss it. I mean, obviously? He shook his head.

Jordan's cell phone was acting strange and didn't alert them that their destination was approaching but he saw the exit number the benefactor had mentioned. Off the highway, they found themselves on the coastline, a long and sometimes walled exterior, gigantic houses looking over the bluffs. The sand stretched for miles below.

Jesus, Imtiaz said, impressed. Even Nathan seemed to wake up from his hangover a little.

Soon a quick right and left on strange one-way streets lined with palm trees, and they came upon a terra cotta wall, and a tall gate with a mounted camera.

Christopher rolled down the window, poked out his head. Uh, guys, he said, unsure what to do. But when his head was fully in view of the lens, the gate started to creak. Welcome, athletes, a mechanical voice said.

Slowly they entered the compound, all four of them staring out their separate windows. It was dense and jungle-like, surprising trees jutting out of the earth. Jordan had the impulse to take a machete to the lot. There was the sound of buzzing insects, and through Christopher's open window the muggy heat rolled over them, as their car slowly followed the narrow but well-groomed road.

Here and there, paths darted out into the brush. But mostly, they twisted and turned in the jungle, so that they began to lose sense of the size of the compound, which had to be quite large, and time. This is awesome, Jordan said again, meaning it this time more in the literal sense of the word.

There was a clearing approaching—a large flat house in that way of Florida accommodations. A sign said The Locker Room in fancy script. It seemed to Jordan that this must be their destination. But as Christopher slowed the car, Jordan noticed the smaller print underneath, which said Stadium with an arrow directing them down the road. He pointed to it, so Christopher kept driving. And then the jungle truly broke, for a boxy cement structure, which Jordan took to be the gym, and, next to it, with the trees falling away and the sea extending as far as any of them could see, a perfect surface. Empty. Lights above, a full three point line, extra hoops on the side, a hybrid form of asphalt made to look like wood. The showcase court.



They each had their own rooms, there seemed to be an endless hallway of them on the first floor. Changed quickly, went back the way they came, jogged together over the gravel path to the courts.

It was full night. Small lanterns next to the path lit the way. The air was cool and heavy. Exhilarated, Jordan found that he was running faster than perhaps he normally would.

Easy there, Imtiaz said from behind.

Typically they stretched before and after, but they were too excited to delay business. The skylights clicked on as they approached. Christopher began speculating appreciatively on what kind of appliances their benefactor had installed to do the trick. Nice camera, he added, pointing at the nearest light: tight security. Suddenly Jordan saw a flash go by him—it was Nathan, sprinting to the far end of the court, a strange sound keening from him, which ended in a shout when he got to the other end.

This is paradise, Imtiaz said.

The lights extended a little away from the court proper, so they could see just the outline of the surf, black and angry against the beach.

They got right to it—shot around for a few minutes, testing the angles on the glass backboards, noting the spongy give of the ground. Christopher posited it was to help water filtration. They admired the nets, brand new cord.

They checked the ball—as always, Jordan and Imtiaz on defense first, Jordan keeping his body in front of wide and sturdy Christopher, doing what he could to prevent from being backed down. Christopher scored two points quickly on jumpers and Jordan was just smiling.

What's up, Christopher asked.

This is so good, Jordan said, gesturing at the glass backboards, the cushioned benches, the waves.

They warmed up. Imtiaz made three banked shots before Nathan adjusted, giving him less space. Jordan found an opening for a give and go. He later committed a hard foul on a driving Nathan. Christopher helped him up. Imtiaz had late-game heroics that Christopher matched, so the game was tied at 15. They played win by two, always. This one was completed relatively quickly at 21, Jordan and Imtiaz taking the opener. Christopher lay on the floor gasping after the final point.

Then he was laughing. Jordan went over to see if he was all right, while the others went to the bench in search of water (it was there, in an ice-filled cooler that had been waiting for them).

It's so simple, Christopher said. Like, why can't we do this always? We could stay here forever.

Later, Jordan overheard him in their well-apportioned but monastic rooms speaking quietly to his wife and daughter. Yes it's fine honey, it's really nice, we'll have to come down here again someday.

The morning was fog and cinnamon. They slumbered through a quick but drowsy game to 11, just to get the kinks out, pre-coffee. Back to the residence to make bacon, all before eight A.M.

The food was already in the refrigerator for them. There was no note or any further explanation on what they could or couldn't take, so they didn't ask questions. Nathan was a chef in addition to a bartender, or so he liked to think of himself, watched cooking shows on mornings off when nine-to-fivers went to work, practiced his craft on himself and friends.

Can you imagine, said Imtiaz, having so much money that you'd just stock all this and let people join?

Well, said Christopher, I try to do my big donations before tax season, and—

I know what you mean man, Jordan interjected, shooting Christopher a look.

It was the often unspoken thing between them, money, which he and Christopher had and Nathan and Imtiaz didn't. Perhaps that was why they didn't split the teams that way. It would have felt too existential, too raw. Well, Nathan did okay ultimately, what with big tips on holidays and the fact that he'd somehow lucked into a rent-controlled apartment in the East Village, lived there through periods even when the landlord shut off hot water. Imtiaz often had more promising things going on—a period as a special ed teacher, pension included, but he left that after three; a while as a deli worker in a Bronx Key Food until he found something more lucrative in administration at NYU. He lost that too, simply because he'd gotten tired of his boss, who he said didn't know how to manage people and was a tiny bit racist, so he skipped out and blew his savings on a few-months trip through South America that he rarely talked about but was always there shining between them. Then again, he didn't have the alimony problems that Nathan had, a former girlfriend and daughter living in Ronkonkoma, who he said it was too hard to visit given the LIRR.

Christopher didn't have much of a concept of their money worries— he'd been employed steadily in various engineering firms for the past decade. He spent little. He'd had a nest egg put aside for his daughter since she was one. It was Jordan who truly stood between the two sides, as an advertising graphics associate, a job he'd lucked into about six years ago when he'd still been a schoolbus driver, dreaming about nothing, nightmares about the fucking kids' happy screams every morning at 5:30. There was a citywide strike and he never looked back. It wasn't

156 often that you started in the mail room for ad agencies anymore but he'd basically done it. He'd always had a talent for design.

Now, he and Christopher had various sources of income, money socked away in a couple places in case something bad befell them or their families. Of course this didn't mean they were happy. But it helped.

One Tuesday morning, a few months before, after they'd finished a particularly tight game at the gym while the benefactor, perhaps, looked over the edge down at them, Imtiaz said, fuck, that was good, let's play another. Christopher and Jordan looked at the gym clock, big and foggy with grime under the glass, but the minute hand ticked on anyway. It was Christopher who said it. Ah I wish, but I gotta get to work.

Imtiaz shrugged. Well, I'm staying. My boss can go fuck himself. Imtiaz was at that point selling cell phones at an AT&T place on Fulton Street.

Of course Christopher wasn't able to help himself. He said: Don't you think that's a bad idea financially?

Imtiaz said loudly: He's not gonna do shit to me. He's not in charge of my life.

He let the ball drop from his hand, went outside the gym door to the water fountain. The ball bounced.

Christopher exchanged a glance with Jordan, shrugged and started changing into his shower shoes, Jordan caught in between. When Imtiaz returned, though, it was Nathan who said, I'll stay with you Im. I've got nothing goin on until seven. And who knows, maybe I blow that off too.

Jordan, who had once been told that he had elements of a protective mother hen in him, looked regretfully behind as he exited. They were still there when he and Christopher got out of the showers, walked past the gym again on their winter morning walk to the train and to work. Christopher was already talking about some new system his office mate was pioneering for use in a semi-industrial live-work space, but Jordan

was thinking about his life choices. What is time? What is free will? **157**
How does it feel to experience regret? The next day Nathan mentioned
that they'd played for four hours, but that was all he said about it. It
was left to Jordan to imagine the aches in the legs, the happy tired, the
dried and reanimated and dried again sweat. The long day's expanse
and perhaps a leisurely coffee or Gatorade. He had only pulled himself
away from the computer screen at eight P.M.

They didn't have these problems of hours at the benefactor's house.
Friday morning, the whole weekend dragged in front of them, an endless
stretch. They watched the end of *Space Jam* and half of an old finals
game on ESPN Classic. The living room television was movie-screen-
size, the air conditioning high. When they'd digested and walked out
into the still-morning for another game, the heat smacked them like
an unseen pick.

Still, they played twos. For some reason Nathan wasn't on his
game for this round, and Christopher wasn't really enough of a scorer
to win a game alone. Imtiaz exhibited his typically fine footwork, even
made Nathan look silly on one crossover occasion. Jordan hit enough
mid-range jumpers not to make it embarrassing. They won by eight.

Afterward, Nathan announced he was taking a break—it was too
hot to play another. He had a point. The sun was now at its height, and
the mugginess had continued unabated. Jordan realized that he was a
little lightheaded, and put his head between his legs to recover. When
he looked up, Nathan had already headed back for the compound. He
and the others trailed behind.

They only caught him as he was coming out the door, a cooler in
hand. Where'd you find that, Christopher asked. Kitchen, Nathan said
shortly. There were bubbles of perspiration beading off the edges. It
looked full. Nathan was wearing a bathing suit.

See you down there, if you want? he asked, and headed for the beach.

 Christopher announced a nap was in order for him, though Jordan imagined it might be just an excuse to call his wife again. Imtiaz disappeared down the hallway, exploring the house. Jordan had a feeling about what Nathan was up to, didn't want to leave him alone.

He found the cooler under an umbrella on the empty beach, ringed a quarter mile in each direction by rock barriers, so that other than them the beach was empty. Nathan was in the water, floating on his back, farther out than looked necessarily safe. Jordan took off his sweaty jersey and laid it down for a seat, next to two drained Coronas, carefully dug into the sand. He started putting on sunscreen that he'd found in one of the cupboards, and kept an eye on Nathan. The calm waves raised his friend up and lowered him out of sight from time to time, but then raised him visible again, his arms stretched out to either side.

Eventually Nathan came out. How ya doin', Jordan asked. He'd never been one who'd been able to sit in what people call "companionable silence."

Nathan didn't answer. He reached into the cooler and pulled out another Corona, took a sip. If it seemed to Jordan that the sip signaled moderation, a good thing in his opinion, he was mistaken. Nathan dropped down to sit under the umbrella and then tilted the bottle up to the sky. It took its neat, empty place next to the other two.

Sometimes it occurred to Jordan that they never really talked about anything, the four of them. Well, plans and so forth, and remembrances of games and hangouts past, but only rarely did they discuss important matters. Clear the air. There had been the era in their early twenties, for example, when Nathan had simply disappeared. They had graduated from college, were all back in the city, eager (or at least this was how Jordan felt at the time—he was eager) to get the crew back together again. But Nathan wouldn't return texts or calls. When he did, it was only to say that he couldn't make it this time, next time folks. It became a dispiriting regularity, and at first they made jokes about it, "next time folks" peopling their text message chains. Eventually they speculated about what was the matter with him, Christopher the one who came up with the obvious, that he was sick. It never occurred to any of them that their friendship might just be gone.

But perhaps Christopher was right, because one evening Nathan did meet them, on a street corner by Times Square where they'd all gathered for a night of drinks, woohoo party, spend whatever cash was in your wallet and don't leave your credit card at the bar. They included Nathan on the text thread because they always did, it was the way with them, probably due to Jordan who didn't like to lose people. They didn't hear from him but then he showed up, on the corner just as they were about to leave it. Hey gang, he said nonchalantly, like regular, like things were totally fine. But he looked thinner than he ever had before, a little haggard, whiter in the face and even his hair seemed less full and fluffy than usual—he was a diminished man. They dapped and hugged and sized him up in somewhat stunned silence, until he finally answered the unspoken questions (or at least half an answer), and said he'd been laid low for a while there with an unusual infection he'd received in the hospital one evening in Nashville (when had he been in Nashville, they asked but didn't find out) and only now was he really able to get around easily on two feet. It was Jordan who asked if he wanted to do something lower-key than a bar, maybe just go to the movies down the block instead. No, he said, the bar. They went, and that was the first time Jordan ever saw anyone that size or age drink six shots successively, and not really seem particularly worse for the wear. I've developed a high tolerance, Nathan said after the fifth, signaling for the sixth. They had a good time that night.

Jordan watched Nathan watching the water. He hoped he wouldn't reach for another Corona. It wasn't that Nathan got angry as much as

**160**  glassy, like not really there. His heart sank as Nathan opened the cooler again, grasped for a bottle. You gonna be alright to play this afternoon, Jordan tried lamely. Don't make it easy for us, he added. Ha.

Nathan's hand stopped scrabbling. He withdrew it. Yeah, he said. You're right. Maybe I should just chill.

Jordan's self-worth ballooned a little there under the umbrella. He kept thinking for the right thing to say, but then Nathan said it.

There's something healthy about beach living, don't you think? Like it can get all the toxins out of us. The city, our crappy lives.

Then Nathan told a story that Jordan hadn't heard before, that apparently Nathan had spent a few months in Hawaii during that sickness period, before it got really bad but after he kind of broke with them. He was bartending at a tourist place, learned the natural surf spots with the locals, went camping full weeks when he felt like it, had some other sucker fill in. He liked watching the real surfers there in the half morning when he was getting off shift, them just starting as the darkness lifted at four, five A.M.

Some days there, Nathan said, I didn't drink at all. He left it at that.

That's good, I guess, Jordan said. Nathan looked at him strangely.

Yeah, he said. But you don't have to be so high minded about it. Don't you ever do anything wrong?

And Jordan thought for a second, but couldn't come up with anything. This put him in a low mood.

A rainstorm came and went and dissipated some of the heat. They found that the basketball court was fully dry moments after, somewhat magically, so they played.

This time Imtiaz wasn't his usual stellar self—actually he was downright awful. It almost seemed that he'd forgotten his skills. He kept bumping into Jordan when Jordan went to set a pick, and following him into the corner with the ball when Jordan was just trying to draw his defender away, give him space. Finally, when they were down 5-1 **161** with their only score being a weak layup Imtiaz had almost missed even though it had been airballed directly into his open hands, Jordan decided to take over. It was a strangely freeing feeling. He'd never really done it before, in all their hundreds of games. He had always been the secondary player, willing to pass, play good defense, give up the shot. Sure, sometimes he made beautiful delicate needlepoint passes, and even scored a three now or then when he was on his game. But mostly, he was supplemental.

Deep down, Jordan had always felt that this was a serious failing within him, that his basketball mediocrity—some might call it steadiness but truly, it was mediocrity—was at the base of the way he lived his life. He knew he had the skills to shoot and score. He could be creative with or without the ball. He had a decent euro step move in the lane that rarely got used. What was stopping him, what planetary force, what failure of mind? It was a lack of courage.

He wasn't sure if other people recognized this, maybe they did, but he had always known it deep within. He was not a brave man.

Funny to count bravery with how one performed on a civilized basketball court. But in this latter day of theirs, it was one of the few chances he had. He had failed in other contexts. Never tested like his father in Vietnam or his grandfather in Europe. He had never had any impulse to do anything but regular jobs, ran away from fires, not toward them. About four years ago, not long after he'd married his wife, they'd been walking down the street from a dinner date and a haggard looking man had crazy-eyed his way up to them walking in the opposite direction. Bitch, he screamed, pointing at Jordan's wife. You're a bitch! His hands were mute and glowing, his face a terrible mask. It seemed to Jordan that the man's pocket had a telltale bulge. Jordan kept walking, pulling his wife after him, not making eye contact with the aggressor.

162 But the man kept screaming at them. And he followed for half a block before leaving them alone.

At first Jordan tried to ignore it, talk about something else, but his wife had removed her hand from his pocket. What, he said, what's wrong. Nothing, she insisted. He knew she was going to make him say it. I didn't defend you.

Even later that night and for the weeks afterward that he spent meditating on the event, he didn't like his other options, which of course he'd considered, mulled, seen through to their natural conclusion, passed over, all within the few moments of the encounter and then for what felt like lifetimes afterward. He could have turned to the man, shielded his wife, said something strong and cognizant—watch your goddamn mouth, etc. He could have simply given the man a stare, put his hands in his own pockets, made it clear he was ready to defend himself and his. But he hadn't. There were outcomes that could have resulted from those decisions, improbable ones, but ones he wasn't sure he was ready to face. He had never seen himself as the alpha man. This mentality, it's true, carried over to the basketball court.

But something turned inside him, at least briefly, or maybe it was forever, in that game when they were down 5–1. It was a mental switch, nothing more. It started when, rather than move off to the wing once he had dumped the ball to Imtiaz after a check, Jordan charged for the hoop. And he wanted the ball, for maybe the first time ever, truly wanted it, rather than 70 percent hoping Imtiaz would keep it for himself. Ball, he called harshly, and Imtiaz gave it to him. Christopher had his girth and wide arms in their usual position, perhaps he figured Jordan would do as he usually did and pass the ball back outside. But he didn't. He stutter-stepped, put his shoulder down into Christopher's chest, reared up and made the basket.

The other three stopped, considering (it seemed to Jordan) what had just happened. If true, it had changed the dynamics of their game. Damn, Imtiaz said, that was dope. Yeah for real, nice shot, added Nathan. Christopher was still nursing his pride/chest. Their reaction only made Jordan more indignant, more shameful, more aware of his usual lack of bravery. Come on, check, he said disdainfully, not accepting their praise, and when he got the ball back he decided to double down. He pumpfaked at the elbow, crossed over into the lane, spun to his left hand (which he'd always felt was his weak hand, as many times as he practiced it on his own) and made the shot.

This happened with some regularity until they were a point away from winning the game.

It was a stunning sensation. Jordan had never experienced anything like it. The wind blowing in off the beach seemed to lift him up. He was strong. He was fearless. When he took it to the backboard for that final score, it was Christopher again who was the last defender, didn't stand a chance in this new era of Jordan's ascendance, Jordan's hand about to float out the ball. And then Jordan felt himself flat on his back, the thud from the back of his head after Christopher shoved him to the ground.

Whoah whoah whoah, Imtiaz was shouting, what the hell was that man. What the fuck.

Just playing defense, said Christopher whinily. But then he was cowering backward, because a strange presence was in his face. It was Jordan.

Jordan found that he was screaming. What was he screaming? He wasn't entirely sure. But he was cursing at Christopher. And then, in what for him was truly a new experience, he palmed his friend with the hard block of his lower hand, right in Christopher's chest.

Christopher was sucking in air. Now Imtiaz was pulling Jordan away. What the hell man, Nathan was shouting. Yo, you okay, Imtiaz asked. He was talking to Christopher, holding Jordan. Damn man, said

**164**  Christopher weakly, his deer eyes looking at Jordan, you knocked the wind outta me. His lip curled a little and a roll of fat puckered under his chin, or at least it seemed like that's what was happening when Christopher bent his head. The sight brought Jordan back to earth. I'm sorry, I'm so sorry. Jesus I dunno what came over me. What the hell. He put an arm over Christopher's shoulder and Christopher warily accepted.

Later that evening, they were back in the main house getting dinner together. Or rather, Nathan was cooking, Imtiaz was icing, and Christopher was calling home. Jordan, feeling guilty about his earlier behavior, was trying to be helpful. The intensity of the experience had gone to his head, and he still felt a little high off it. He reached for a second beer in the well-stocked refrigerator to calm himself down.

You want one, he asked Nathan. Nah, Nathan said.

Jordan looked at him curiously. Cool man, was all he said.

Nathan stopped his chop of the fresh garlic that had been available to them in the pantry. You know, he said. Then he stopped. Forget it.

But Jordan waited.

Isn't it strange, Nathan started again a few seconds later, how everyone is acting a little off down here. I mean, it's only Friday night, but I've seen some things I never thought I'd see.

Like what, Jordan said slowly.

Well, there's me and my drinking, said Nathan. I just don't have the taste for it here.

He ticked off his fingers. Imtiaz isn't playing worth a shit. I've never seen him so lackluster and easy to defend, even before the last game where you took over. And then you…

Jordan saved him the embarrassment. Yeah, he said. Kind of lost my temper there. He looked down quietly at his hands, trying to indicate that he felt bashful about it. In reality, he didn't. Not at all.

But Christopher, he said finally. Christopher is just like normal. Windows-sales-conference-wifey.

Yeah I guess so, Nathan shrugged. Whatever. Just thought it was a little weird.

They ate dinner, another fabulous meal that Nathan had pulled together out of, it seemed to Jordan, pots, pans, and nothing. As usual Nathan insisted in his prideful but quiet way that the ingredients he needed had all been there waiting for him, almost as if he had ordered them. Jordan was nearly doubled over with fullness from the fourth taco he'd eaten, just to have something to do with his hands—he was really unbelievably anxious, itchy, excited (he now saw) to get out on the court. Imtiaz had already made it clear that he wanted the night off from games, rest his legs and brain. He was in a satisfied mood though, he'd gotten enough Wi-Fi for a second to see that his boss at the phone store had emailed him about a raise coming, and he'd found a funny picture in the living room of another set of four guys like them in basketball shorts, maybe left behind by other of the benefactor's visitors. Goofy as hell man, Imtiaz said, and it was true—one was fat, one was skinny and tall, one had an emo-looking wave to his hair, the other was staring into the distance of the baskeball court like one lost. The others had laughed about who was who in their crew but still didn't express interest in a night game. So Jordan could only curb his energy by eating so much that he'd never be able to lift a leg.

When they were done, Jordan having cleaned up much of the kitchen with Christopher, Christopher straightened out his shirt, which Jordan now realized was a neat-looking button down.

Hey I know it's a little off-topic, Christopher said, but do you have any interest in going out on the town tonight? I mean, you know, we're here. We don't get away every day.

All Jordan really wanted to do was benefit from his newfound

166  killer bball instinct, but considering how much of a d-bag he'd been to Christopher that afternoon he knew that he had to say yes. They went into the gigantic living room together, where the others were watching a late-season meaningless Celtics game. Christopher made his pitch, but then faltered when he realized they'd have to drive somewhere, a departure from normal life in New York. They were a few drinks in. That's okay, said Nathan, I'll drive. I haven't had any.

They didn't really know where they were going. They might have looked up a destination or at least a general area on their cell phones, but since their arrival none of them had had consistent signal this far out in the boonies, Christopher said even his short call home had been grainy and then dropped. Instead they followed their instincts. They passed a few likely strip mall spots with what looked like utilitarian bars, or even large Applebees-type establishments whose windows were coated with perspiration whether from the breaths of many people or too much air conditioning they did not know. Here, Christopher said when they saw a particular sign on the highway, it had passed too quickly for Jordan to notice. When they pulled into the parking lot Jordan saw: Cheaters.

Jordan wasn't sure what made him more uncomfortable: the fact that Christopher had picked the spot in the first place or that Nathan and Imtiaz got out of the car without a hesitation or word. They walked with Christopher toward the strip club's dark entrance, Nathan turning back momentarily to lock the door on the rental. He saw that Jordan was still standing by the side. You coming, he asked?

They were inside and Jordan had bad memories of all the other times he'd been in strip clubs. The stupid college trip to Montreal. The bachelor party for his sister's first husband. Once, on his own dumb accord off the West Side Highway before his fine marriage, when he was at a real bottom of the barrel moment regarding romance, as if the neon lights and sparkles on bare oiled skin would heal him. He left on that occasion in ten minutes, went home and showered. The smell of the place, its steak and vodka, stayed on him for days and it came back when he walked by at lunchtime for the next few weeks. This place was more of the same. The long bar and the dim lights, the seven or eight patrons, heads bent down while their eyes looked up, taking in whatever they were taking in.

As they settled in at a table Jordan ordered a whiskey on the rocks. He did it angrily, and when it came, he slugged it back. He banged his hand on the table when the waitress, herself a beautiful woman who in some ways was more the kind of person Jordan was looking for than any of the women more obviously presenting themselves, sent him a scathing look. Yo chill man, Imtiaz said, generously putting down a twenty for the drink.

I'm just trying to get a sip, said Jordan.

In fact he became so preoccupied with staring down the waitress and getting that drink, and stewing over whatever b.s. reason he was being dragged to this place at all, that he didn't realize that Nathan and Imtiaz were no longer paying attention to him, that they were watching Christopher in something approaching horror, and that Christopher was fully preoccupied himself. He was just a face and a balding crown and all hands, he'd always had large hands even when they were teenagers, hands searching themselves like spiders up and down one of the dancers' bodies. All Jordan could see was her legs.

Is he okay, Jordan said quietly, still feeling that anger within him and hoping for another drink though the sensation was slightly diminished.

Nathan shook his head. He opened his mouth to say something, but at that moment the dancer shifted her position, turned around to face Christopher so that her breasts were in his face. They saw only her back. Jordan noticed that a small birth mark had been covered

168 over perhaps accidentally with some of the glitter. He almost wanted to touch it, to wipe the glitter away. The woman's body gyrated, and Christopher leaned his head back.

Yes, Christopher said. Finally.

Then he whispered in the woman's ear. She nodded, put one hand on his leg. Christopher's body moved too, a slow grind, nothing like the fleetness of foot that he sometimes displayed on the basketball court. He staggered after her. But he did follow her, when she disappeared behind a door in the back of the room.

He returned ten minutes later.

He was smiling. His chest was thrown forward, his hands, so often confined to pockets, it seemed to Jordan, were swaying confidently at his sides. He sat down with them once again. They hadn't spoken since he left.

His brimming overflowed. Guys, he said, what happened to us way back when? It's all coming back to me now. That woman, she reminded me so much of Diane. Where is she? How far away was that? Do you think we can go back?

Diane. Jordan did remember Diane. How could he forget. The type of girl that dropped the participation rate in a high school classroom just by attending. Jordan had English with her, still remembered the old purple sweatshirt she wore most days of the week, it clung just enough to be tantalizing. She was far out of his league but that seemed to be true for everyone, so she was equally friendly to the true high school stars—their actual basketball players and drummers—and people like him, who just *were*.

It came back to him, the night of their junior prom, to which Christopher had gone dateless and wearing a funny bow tie. In fact, Christopher and Jordan had gone "together," whatever that meant, as neither of them had dates and they didn't want to be standing around alone. Of course what it really meant was that it was the two of them, 169 plus Imtiaz and his girlfriend from the neighborhood, plus Nathan and the woman who would be the mother of his daughter in two years, that year they were still speaking. And they all piled into Imtiaz's dad's car, loaned for the night, this was before drinking, or at least before drinking for them, and yet they were having such a good time, Jordan couldn't exactly remember why, maybe the song that had come over the radio or the fact that they always enjoyed themselves, the four of them together. Diane of course was the first person they encountered in the fifth floor fire trap their school's junior prom committee had wrangled up from somewhere in pre-Craigslist New York. They had all been laughing at something Nathan said, he was always trying to make them and the future mother of his child laugh, perhaps that's why they stayed together for the length of time that they did, and that's when Diane saw them, and perhaps they looked more alluring than they did in real life. Or perhaps it was never having seen them before in suits and ties, and they looked sharp, the suits took away the usual youthful affectations, they looked ready for the world. Christopher especially, his natural thick-boned-ness not yet having given way to thickness, the girth that in middle age would sag slightly, but years before, he suddenly looked significant, confident, large. Hey Diane, he said, with the air of someone throwing themselves off a ledge, and to all of their great surprise, she turned toward them: her blue-black dress, tightly pulled-back hair, sliver of neck, swath of back, lips thin and smiling and accentuated by, Jordan didn't know, makeup he guessed. She beamed. You boys look great, she said, as if she were worlds ahead of them already.

But by some premonition, by some hint of fate, maybe it was a bargain with the devil, because Christopher truly would never reach it again—he knew the words, they came to him, he stepped into his role. He offered her his hand. Said coolly, confidently, maturely: You look

170 beautiful Diane. Never change.

Something shifted in her face when she heard this. Something seemed to both give up and be decided. It was as if she heard a voice from her future (Jordan remembered he'd heard how things had gone for her, she was a mother of three in Arizona, where somebody she went to college with now worked for a bank. In Facebook pictures she did in fact still look like she did then, or maybe she was using an old Facebook picture, or maybe she was stuck). But maybe she didn't know back on that prom night whether never changing would be good or bad, or if like a perfectible spin move on the basketball court she would be performing the same motion, over and over, for the rest of her life.

She spent the evening with them. She added a jewel to their little circle, an element of something special. And always, she stayed near Christopher, and toward the end of the night Jordan watched her turn to him, her head tilted backward like a smile, and Christopher leaned forward, he kissed her neck.

That night they were all sleeping in Imtiaz's basement, and they heard Christopher's first experiments with sex despite the bathroom radio he had turned on, quietly, to Z100. The techno pulse only serving to accentuate the whispers from the room, which all would claim the next morning they hadn't heard though for Jordan at the very least this wasn't true. Imtiaz was off in the one corner cuddling with his girlfriend, Nathan with his, but they were far enough away and perhaps experienced sufficiently at subterfuge that all he heard was Christopher, or rather the sounds of things in the bathroom moving—a squeak on the floor, a bang of perhaps a hand on the wall, the water accidentally turned on and then giggling, and then soft whispering, and then quiet. Only once, at the very end, a soft moan, and though Jordan couldn't be sure he had always assumed it was Christopher.

They drove back to the compound. Jordan prepared for Christopher to be upset, ashamed, embarrassed, and he had all the things ready that he would say to him, but those things flew out of his mind because Christopher apparently felt nothing of the sort.

What a night, he repeated over and over as the highway scenery repeated in front of their eyes. It all rolled into one for Jordan, so that he became dizzy. What a, what a night.

Then: I can't believe how good that felt, he said.

Dude, Jordan said, looking to the others. Nathan was calmly driving, Imtiaz curled up in the front seat, eyes almost closed. He looked back, rolled his eyes and shrugged.

Christopher looked at Jordan curiously. What?

What the fuck is wrong with you man, Jordan said.

Christopher leaned back as far as he could from Jordan, which wasn't far in the back seat of their rented car. Perhaps Jordan had been shouting. What the fuck's wrong with *you*? Christopher spit back.

You're so over the top down here. We're on vacation bro. Jesus.

You have a kid man, Jordan said. What the fuck are you doing going to a strip club. Is this what you do on all those work conferences.

As a matter of fact sometimes I do, Christopher said monumentally. What do you care what I do with my own time. That's no one's business but mine and my wife's.

Then his voice dropped a little, and he smiled wickedly. But it feels even better down here than it ever has before, I'll tell you that, he said.

They came to the exit, went through the gates, Nathan guiding the car slowly along the gravel. Jordan occupied his mind with restraining himself from punching a hole through the window, or trying to. They parked in front of the big house. Before Nathan could even kill the engine, shut off the air conditioning, Jordan said, let's play.

They changed quickly into basketball clothes. Jordan was done first, didn't wait for the others. He ran down the gravel path through the

172 jungle to the court, feeling his body begin to wake up from toes to neck. He felt sore at first, wasn't sure he would be able to do much more than limp, but soon the beauty of lactic acid leaving the body began to thrill him, and toward the end of the path he was sprinting. A wind from the east brought the chop of the sea. The sky was pitch black above him, until Jordan turned on the lights and it may as well have been day. He took a basketball from the plastic locker at courtside, began to shoot.

They didn't say anything when they arrived, the others, just took their own balls from the locker and dribbled. Soon they began. Nathan checked the ball to Imtiaz, and then promptly stole it back. Before completing the layup, Nathan paused a little, as if to say, something had to have been a mistake there, as if to give it back. Grab it, Jordan bellowed at Imtiaz. But even the hesitation and the exhortation didn't make anything click enough for Imtiaz to return to former glory. He was staring at his hands, as if they had let him down for the first time. Something was glowing. And as Nathan shrugged a little, took the hop step to the hoop to make the open layup, something happened on the far side of the court which was that Jordan seemed to move from one place to the other, not within time but as if he were, briefly, in both places at once. He was at the hoop and in the air and rising, batted Nathan's layup away. He did not bat it down. He was so high, so powerful, that the ball kept rising, kept going, over the evergreen-decorated fence and into the wind stream, at the edge of the cliff. It seemed that by the time Jordan landed, only then did they hear the splash.

Jordan hit the balls of his feet. He was breathing hard, his senses overloaded.

What the hell is going on man, Nathan mumbled. Something's happening down here. I feel like everyone's going haywire, I think I want to go home. Jordan laughed, a high angry cackle he didn't recognize. You're just mad, he said. Just mad I figured out how to beat you all.

All of you. No, Nathan said. This is different. But he checked the ball. And Jordan hardly gave the ball to Imtiaz at all other than to perform the customary courtesy pass. He took over; he dominated; he laid his friends to waste.

It didn't feel as good as Jordan thought it would when it ended, 16-1. He had always wondered, is this what it would be like? Is this what the worldbeaters felt? He had never had those dreams that children have of becoming warriors, or president, or famous. But here it was and something felt metallic inside him, harder and more authoritative. He opened his mouth and realized it was blood.

Suddenly the hot muggy air settled on them all, and they stared at one another in a stupor at half court, not able to speak.

I need water, Nathan gasped. I'm so thirsty.

I can't see too well, said Imtiaz.

What's happening, Christopher asked soulfully.

I don't know, Jordan said.

But then they saw it—over the top of the indoor basketball court a cloud, a curtain, a mass of flies buzzing viciously—no, a helicopter landing out of the dark and endless sky. The sand swirled around them, and then the dust, and the court became one with the beach and the forest, and Jordan wondered if they'd ever be able to play again. Of course they would. Oh, they would. They had not known with whom they were dealing. They had not known how little they'd be able to help themselves; how they were trapped. They stood as one, in a line, as the sounds stopped and the dust fell and vision was restored to them all. And they waited for the helicopter's tines to stop turning, and the helicopter hatch to fall open, the suited man to emerge from within, arms crossed and ready to watch the eternal contest—their benefactor returned to claim his terrible and just reward. <

*Mark Chiusano is the author of* Marine Park: Stories *(Penguin). His fiction has been published in* Guernica, Narrative, Harvard Review, *and elsewhere.*

# PENELOPE REWORKS HER THREADS

LISA HIGGS

Say I was faithful.

Say I was clever enough
to hold a rock
watered on all sides
to benefit your name.

Say I knew your faith
rested between your legs.
Say your tears wet your cheeks
like any child's.

Say among men, you thought
of me.

Say I am a liar.

Say I was faithful,
The only option
for a woman bound to a man
wily as you.

My tears burned
like wax down the night candle.
Among women, I thought
many things not you.

There are battles and battles.
Say the killing kind carries
more import.

Say monsters make the better myth.



I was faithful
to my chance of immortality.

The weeping wife who survives.

Say I proved my need of you.
You would not be wrong.

Your name lost served me better.

Say I am a liar.
I was clever enough
to craft decades to my advantage.

The indefinite wait gave more
worth than the return.

# THE PATTERNS OF HISTORY
## A CONVERSATION WITH MARGARET WILKERSON SEXTON

### JOHN McMURTRIE

Had her passion for fiction not taken over, Margaret Wilkerson Sexton's writing might have been confined to drafting legal memos and briefs. Instead, the New Orleans-raised daughter of lawyers left her career in the law to chart her own path—as a novelist. In the handful of years since, Sexton, who now lives in Oakland, has written two novels that have received high praise. *A Kind of Freedom,* published in 2017, was long-listed for the National Book Award. *The Revisioners,* which came out last fall, made The New York Times' 100 Notable Books of 2019.

Published by Counterpoint Press of Berkeley, both novels take a panoramic and personal approach to telling stories of African American families in New Orleans over great stretches of time. *A Kind of Freedom* brings readers into the lives of three generations, alternating among 1944, 1986, and 2010. The sweep of *The Revisioners* is even broader, extending from 1855 to 2017. Interracial tension fuels much of its plot, as in the contemporary section, when Ava, a young African American woman who has landed on hard times, decides to move in with Martha, her benevolent but prejudiced grandmother, who is white. With the discipline that she applied to her legal writing, Sexton relates her characters' struggles with sober precision, heightening the tension without resorting to melodrama.

In an interview over brunch at Brown Sugar Kitchen, a soul-food restaurant in downtown Oakland, Sexton talked about her early writing, her interracial marriage, and her thoughts on the changing demographics of the Bay Area. She was solicitous, asking almost as many questions as her interlocutor, laughing easily, and with a big smile. After brunch, she displayed her first tattoo, which she had just acquired the day after turning thirty-seven. The cursive handwriting on her arm belongs to her Great-Aunt Louise. It reads, "Freedom."

**JOHN MCMURTRIE:** Tell me about how you came to be a writer. You studied creative writing at Dartmouth, but what got you interested in writing in the first place?

**MARGARET WILKERSON SEXTON:** I always wanted to do it. Starting from the age of eight or so. We had an assignment at school to write a poem, and I wrote the poem, and it was easy to write. My dad read it and he said, "This is a very special poem. You're really good at this." And I think it was just getting the affirmation from my dad, and loving that affirmation. And I enjoyed it. So I just started thinking and saying I would be a writer. Of course, I've looked at the poem as an adult, and I don't think there was much special about it [laughs].

**JM:** So you wrote this poem at age eight, and then what?

**MWS:** I was in middle school, in maybe the seventh grade, and I had this English teacher, and she was really the only teacher that showed any special interest in me. Because I think there was a lot of racism in this middle school, in retrospect. There were so few black students, and the administrators and the teachers would confuse us all the time because they weren't accustomed to seeing black people at all. So, this one teacher, my English teacher, actually read passages of an essay [I wrote] out loud to the class. And she said, "My husband

178

teaches writing at a community college and he says he can't get his students to write. And I told him, I have one who can." And honestly, I'll never forget that. But so many writers have these stories about one teacher who made one comment. People don't realize the impact they have. I mean, hearing that, I was like, "Okay, this is a skill that I have. This is like a gift, and I should use that."

So I went to high school, I was at this great boarding school, and they let us do stuff like start our own literary magazine. And they had this initiative where you could do an independent study project. And so I wrote a book.

**JM:** You wrote a book?

**MWS:** Yeah, I wrote a book. It was called *Shadows of Another Day*. And it was about a black woman who married a white guy. I don't even know if they were married. I think she was dating this guy, and she was pregnant. And just the discord that followed in her family because of it, and his family. The fact that they gave me the oppor-

tunity—it made me think I could write a book. It made me think that was a feasible thing.

**JM:** That's impressive. Do you still have that book?

**MWS:** I do, because my mom thinks it should be published. My mom thinks it's really good.

**JM:** Is that going to happen?

**MWS:** No [laughs]. My mom, she's ahead of her time. My grades were pretty good, but they weren't stellar. And so she said, "If you really want to get into a really good school, you need to do something with this writing thing, because that's your thing." And so, I was like, "Okay, I'll write a book." And I did.

**JM:** You got into a good school, Dartmouth. And then you became a lawyer after going to Berkeley Law?

**MWS:** Well, I went to the Dominican Republic for a year after college. And there, I was also supposed to be writing a book. I got this grant to do that, and to work at this civil rights organization. Maybe two weeks after I got there, my grandmother died. And my grandmother almost raised me. We were very close. And so I was grieving. I just wasn't happy. I finished the book, but it was a terrible experience of being in such a solitary profession in that country, because I didn't know anybody. So I decided, maybe it's not for me. And my parents were lawyers, and my dad was at that time heavily encouraging me to go to law school. And so I thought, "Yeah, okay, I'll apply." I did apply, and I got into good schools. And I honestly think that at that time, you can get addicted to that kind of achievement. I think I was like, "This feels like the track I'm used to. I'll just do that." And so I didn't write again for five years.

**JM:** And then what happened? How did you get the bug back?

**MWS:** I was at this law firm at the height of the recession, and we really didn't have much work. And so I would write little essays, I would send them to my friends. And my friends would be like, "Oh, my gosh, this is so good." You

know, that kind of thing. And then one day, they call us all into the conference room—the management has an announcement at this firm. And I basically pack up my desk because I'm certain, we all are, that this is when they're going to tell us we're all laid off. But we go in there, and they have this initiative program that they're laying out where you can leave for a year and pursue your own dreams—they call it "doing pursuits"—and they'll pay you a portion of your salary. And that's better for them than having the stigma of massive layoffs. So I was like, "Oh, man, this is like a sign." Because I hated it. I loved some of the work, but the environment, it was pretty toxic. The screaming, the clichés that we've all heard about law firms, that was actually happening there. So I thought about it, and I was like, "I've only been here a year and a half—it's not enough time if I want to have some kind of legal career." I stayed for another year, and it got worse and worse.

180

And then I got married in October of 2011. And at my wedding, I was sitting there listening to these toasts at the rehearsal dinner. They were all so positive and lovely. And I really internalized them. I actually sat there and I heard them and absorbed them. It just accelerated my path, or lifted my frequency in some way, hearing all these compliments. And I just walked in the next day that I

are set in Louisiana, mostly in New Orleans, where you grew up. Did you always imagine telling the story of that place in your writing?

**MWS:** So, my first book was about an African American girl who goes to the Dominican Republic, and she's trying to help this struggling community, and she ends up harming it before she leaves. It was really about colorism—that was the major theme in

> *"It was really about colorism—that was the major theme in that book. Like the colorism she experienced in New Orleans was being replayed in the Dominican Republic."*

went to work, and I gave notice. And I took the little incentive program. Of course, six months later, they were bankrupt, so I got six months of a portion of my salary. But by then I had written for six months, so I knew that I could do it. And I had the luxury—my husband was working and we didn't have kids at the time.

**JM:** Both of your novels, *A Kind of Freedom* and *The Revisioners,*

that book. Like the colorism she experienced in New Orleans was being replayed in the Dominican Republic. I didn't harm anybody, but it was basically an exaggerated version of what I felt happened when I went to the Dominican Republic. And I really thought that was my story to tell. I really thought that was going to be my breakout book. And then nobody would publish it. But my sister-in-law, she was like, "Oh, my God, your writing! I used to work for a publisher based in Berkeley—we should all get brunch." So we go to this brunch, and it's the publisher and his wife—it's Jack Shoemaker [of Counterpoint Press] and it's Jane Vandenburgh—it's me and it's my sister-in-law, Abby. And three days later, Jane Vandenburgh contacted me, and she's like, "I do this yearlong narrative program, I really think you'd be great for it. And you know, the idea is you send me twenty pages a month, and then by the end of the year, we have a book." And she edits them for you, helps you with whatever you're struggling on with this book. And I was like, "No, I don't think so." I was thinking this because I already have my book, I have the Dominican book. But then I thought about it for a few days. I was like, "Margaret, you truly don't have anything going for you. You have this book that nobody really wants to read."

And I always had it in the back of my mind that my second book would be a book about three generations of a New Orleans family spanning World War II to post-Katrina. It was one of those things where I thought, it's such an easy idea—to me, it was the story of my family. I almost didn't want to give it weight because it felt so easy. And I thought, "Well, that'll be a good little book to write with Jane for this project while I continue to get my breakout book out there." And then after three months, Jane was like, "This is really good. I want to show it to Jack." And I thought, "Okay, if she's going to show it to Jack, I should hurry up and finish it." So, I finished it in maybe four months. No joke.

**JM:** One of the striking things about your novels is how you tell stories of families across generations. This allows the reader to make connections between different eras and see how a character's life in, say, 2010 is a direct consequence of what that person's ancestors went through. There's a lot of historical amnesia in this country, and in linking these time

**182**

periods, jumping back and forth between them, you remind us in an immediate, visceral way that the legacy of slavery persists. How did you arrive at this ambitious narrative approach?

**MWS:** To me, it didn't feel ambitious. It's just the way my mind works, it's just the way to tell the story. Even in other areas, I'm

moments in *A Kind of Freedom* is when one of the young male characters, T.C., gets pulled over by the police. And he knows then and there, because he has some pot in the car, that he's going back to prison. You feel so strongly that the cards have simply been stacked against him, much as he wants to improve his lot in life.

> *"I find that there's historical amnesia even within families—people think that whatever they're going through is so isolated. But if you were able to interview your ancestors, I bet your grandmother went through the same thing."*

always trying to get to the root of a problem. Like if a friend has a problem, I always want to take it back to its original context. And I think that kind of plays out in the writing. I think as I analyze it, it gives the book texture to have all of that additional information for the reader. And it's really neat to see the parallels. I think it shows how little has changed.

**JM:** For me, one of the saddest

**MWS:** There are these systemic forces that are doing that, of course. But I also believe in generational patterns. You said the cards have been stacked against him—it's so true, even in the sense that he's almost reliving his father's life because his father wasn't able to confront those demons. And so now it's on him. I find that there's historical amnesia even within families—people think that whatever they're going through is so isolated. But if you were able to interview your ancestors, I bet your grandmother went through the same thing. Maybe it looked a little different on the surface, but it's like the same kinds of patterns in her life.

**JM:** T.C.'s mother, Jackie, can't help but worry about her son's fate, even when he's just an infant. You capture this when you write, "She didn't know why she felt so certain tragedy lurked in his future. Everything was fine now, and she tried to remind herself of that. She'd grip the edge of the bassinet and wipe her eyes, but the early grief wouldn't budge." This is a worry that can take hold of any parent, but it's a feeling that is especially pronounced for the characters in your narratives.

**MWS:** I hadn't read *A Kind of Freedom* in a very long time, so you reading that was very interesting because I'd forgotten about that sentiment. But I feel it so strongly with my own children, especially my two sons. Not as much my

daughter. My youngest baby is two, I don't worry about him yet. But the six-year-old, because he's in the school system, oh my God, I'm already very vigilant about the way he'll be perceived as a student. Not as much with discipline, because he's well-behaved, but just as a student. I really worry that he'll be underestimated and pigeonholed. And then as they get older, I think the worries change because, you know, as a mom, I have so much control over him now. I know where he is at all times. But I think I've seen from family members and from friends and from what I know about the country, black mothers with black sons, that worry starts creeping in very soon. Like maybe when they're ten, that they'll be perceived as older than they are, that they'll be perceived as threatening and that they'll be harmed by police or by other people.

**JM:** I'm impressed that you published *The Revisioners* only two years after *A Kind of Freedom*—its structure is even more

184 complex than the first novel, and it takes readers back to the mid-nineteenth century. How did this story come about for you?

**MWS:** I was living in the Dominican Republic with my [future] husband, and we were in this bubble before we got there. We were at Dartmouth, and all my friends were black, and he had a very diverse group of friends. And so we really didn't experience racism. We were always on campus, and everybody knew us, and it was pretty safe. Then we got to the D.R., and racism and colorism are pervasive in that country at a whole different level than what I was accustomed to, to be honest. I remember thinking, I can't wait to go back to the U.S. because I'll feel so much safer. People thought that I was Dominican of Haitian descent, and there's terrible racism targeting Dominicans of Haitian descent in that country. My husband, though, because of colonialism, was treated like a king. We know about segregation, we know about racial violence, we know about all of these extreme examples of racial dissonance and racism. But I was like, "How would it infect a couple?"

And then I started meeting his friends and family for the first time. And they were completely lovely, and still are, and yet I really hadn't had a lot of close relationships with white people at that point. And these are people who have become my family members. And yet I'm often aware of the fact that they're white and I'm black. That dynamic doesn't escape me ever. So I just started to think about how I could express the degree to which these old dynamics and the legacy of slavery are still present, even in intimate relationships between people who are married or between a daughter-in-law and a mother-in-law, between friends.

Initially, the book was just going to be an enslavement section and a present-day section. There would be a black woman and a white woman in the present-day section, and a black woman and a white woman in the enslavement section. But I didn't want to do a slave narrative because there have been so many, and they've been done so well, and I just didn't want to invest my energy in a slave narrative. I thought, "Why retraumatize readers if there's no value being added?" So I thought, "Well, what's another angle here?" And I had this vision of this farmer, she's in the 1920s. And I just started playing around with this, and this voice was so clear. Like I just had to transcribe. This lady was just in my head. And so I just went with it, and it worked. So then it was the enslaved section, the 1924 section, and the present-day section.

**JM:** Female characters figure prominently in *The Revisioners.* Did you know people like Martha growing up in New Orleans?

**MWS:** I didn't know anybody like that growing up, but now I do. And when the 2016 election happened, I felt like, "Okay, this really needs to be addressed, this is time-sensitive." Martha is struggling with some kind of dementia-related ailment. Martha's progressive, by all measures. I mean, she's a good person. But I wanted to show how that doesn't necessarily absolve you from whatever your role is in contributing to the system we have now. And I also wanted women [like her] to be presented compassionately, though, because it's a tough situation that they're in as well.

**JM:** Martha is frightening. She can be sweet, but then you see the flip side of her character.

**MWS:** And that's so real. That's been an experience I've had with white women of all ages. I feel like everybody does this, though, to the extent that they have privilege, they want to protect it. We're talking about in this context, but it's a

> *"... I wanted to show how that doesn't necessarily absolve you from whatever your role is in contributing to the system we have now."*

185

**186** very human thing to do. People are fine until they're vulnerable, and then you really see what's going on. And we all do that, you know?

**JM:** There's a lot of heartache in your books, and you cover a lot of deadly serious subjects—the KKK, drug dealing, incarceration, and police violence—but the books maintain a dispassionate voice that makes them all the more powerful.

**MWS:** Thank you for saying that. I really appreciate that. Even as a child, I liked to talk about things that are heavy and maybe heart-breaking. I would ask my mom. For instance, her mother was very sick when I was fifteen or so, and I remember asking her for details about it, which most people don't want to know. I've always been interested in that kind of material. It's just like a fact of life for me. It's easy for me to convey it that way.

**JM:** A traditional American story line is that we're all moving for-ward and progressing as a nation, as a shining democracy. But your books are a reality check on that notion.

**MWS:** That's right, that was the intention of both of those books. There has obviously been so much progress. We have come quite a long way. And I think older people recognize that. But on the other hand, some things really haven't changed. Some things are truly still going on, but the names of them have changed. Like, we had Jim Crow, and now we have mass incarceration. It's the same system at work, but it's called something different. We obviously have so much work to do.

**JM:** Let's talk a bit about the Bay Area and your life here. As you know, San Francisco and Oakland, because of the cost of housing, are becoming less racially diverse. In the 1970s, San Francisco's black population was roughly 13 percent, and it's now about 5 percent. What is life like for you here, coming from New Orleans, where more than half of the city's residents are African American?

**MWS:** I lived [in San Francisco] for three or four years, and I really didn't like San Francisco. I could tell that it was just 5 percent. I didn't know that statistic, but that was obvious to me. My husband and I would go to restaurants, and I'd always be the only black person there. I don't feel good about Oakland in the sense that the changes here are devastating to the city in some ways. But I feel better about Oakland than San Francisco because there's so much more diversity.

Even New Orleans is gentrifying now. I mean, some people call New Orleans the new Brooklyn. In some ways, of course, it's helping the city, and in some ways, it's devastating the history, and it's just like here. I don't think it's to the same degree, of course, but people who live in New Orleans are very concerned about gentrification.

**JM:** What do you miss about New Orleans?

**MWS:** Well, I miss the way I grew up in New Orleans. We lived in New Orleans East, my mom and I. My mom was a single mom, even though my dad lived there. They were divorced. And we lived within walking distance of so many of my first cousins. You don't have to call, you just go. And I really miss that. It was just a really nice childhood, in some ways. My grandmother had seven children, so on Sundays, all of her kids and their kids would get together at our house. I was an only child, but I usually felt like I had these social outlets because I had so many friends who were so close to each other. And I miss having a home—I knew everything about New Orleans. And now I feel like it's hard to actually claim a place. Even though I've been in the Bay Area for thirteen years, I would never say this is my home.

But really, I don't want to ever live in New Orleans. I feel like I get quite enough of it when I visit, especially since my dad passed. I used to enjoy visiting, but since he passed last year, I haven't liked going. But my books are set there, so the book tours start there. I'm bombarded with the memories. I guess it's still early in the grief process.

188

Also, my husband's white, my kids are biracial, and I feel we need to live in a place where there are a lot of biracial kids, so that they don't feel weird about it. And I think we need to live in a place that's pretty, at least on the surface, progressive. I mean, at least people are pretending to be progressive. And so I feel like here, it's pretty common to be in an interracial relationship. We're not going to be challenged on that. And I don't know if I would feel that confidence in New Orleans. I never see interracial couples in New Orleans. I love the familial aspect of New Orleans, but colorism was so prominent in New Orleans, and being a dark-skinned person in New Orleans was very difficult when I was a child. I don't know if it's still the case.

**JM:** And you say you're not quite settled here in Oakland.

**MWS:** Well, I like it here. I mean, I'll always live here. I just don't feel like I have the authority. But I didn't grow up here, and I feel like, "Do I really have permission to tell a story here?" Whereas with New Orleans, because it was my foundational childhood home, I do feel like I do have that authority. You know how childhood is—it's twelve years, but it feels like it's thirty-five years.

**JM:** Are you working on a third book, and can you talk about it?

**MWS:** Yes, this book that I'm working on now, it started out as a short story collection, but the stories are linked. It's about two cousins and their relationship with each other and their marriages and their kids. It's really like an ordinary story about these cousins. It's not tackling major racial issues in the country. But of course race is present, these are black women, and we're going to get into the lives of their parents and their grandparents. To be honest, one of the characters is married to a white man, and that's a story. And actually, one of the issues is that she and her husband are separated for six months, and while they're separated the husband has a relationship with a white woman and gets the woman pregnant. And so then the wife and husband get back together, and the black woman has to raise this white child.

The book after that that I'm really excited about is called *The Roof*. It's an adaptation of *Fiddler on the Roof*, from the perspectives of the daughters, and the daughters are black women. I'm obsessed with *Fiddler on the Roof.*

I've seen it onstage a million times and I watched the movie at home.

It's actually like this revisionist situation where this black preacher leaves his community in the South and goes to this random little enclave in California. And he starts this community and it's just totally insulated from the rest of the country, and it's this black community. And then years later, there are these whites that move into a neighboring area, and the same kind of dynamics start to come into play as *Fiddler on the Roof*, in terms of them trying to take over this little town. But the daughters are getting married— that's the main story.

**JM:** You're prolific.

**MWS:** I try to be. I mean, I feel like I have this little window. I was trying to get published for like ten years, and it wasn't happening. And now I feel like, "Well, at least I have an editor." And I treat it like a job. I don't get into like, "Do I have inspiration today?" I don't do that. When I wrote *A Kind of Freedom*, I only had fifteen hours of child care a week, so I was like, "If you don't do it, that's it, you don't have any more child care." And I very much wanted to be published. I very much wanted it to work out because all of my friends were getting promoted, and that was my standard. And I felt like, "Oh, my God, what am I doing with my life?" So I just took it really seriously. ✄

> "*I'm obsessed with* Fiddler on the Roof. *I've seen it onstage a million times...*"

*John McMurtrie is the former books editor of the* San Francisco Chronicle. *His writing has appeared in* The New York Times, The Boston Globe, Literary Hub, *and* Alta.

# ATITLÁN

## PETER ORNER

She'd gone to Guatemala with another guy. I don't know what happened. I didn't ask. She called me collect, crying. I told my boss my grandmother died.

"Another one? What? You've got five grandmothers?"

"My beloved step-grandmother Swenson who raised me from a pup."

"I should have fired your ass fourteen months ago."

"Before I was hired?"

"Get the fuck out of here."

I took a Taca airlines flight to Guatemala City. The entire flight the overhead bin doors flapped like wings. From Guatemala City, I took a yellow school bus to Antigua. Beautiful old colonial town. Buildings, once white, now sooty. She'd been enrolled in a Spanish immersion course. She dropped out after whatever happened with the guy she went down there with. Buenos dias mi vida. She met me at the bus. That was the year she wore a headband. Her arm was in a sling. I didn't ask about that, either. We took another yellow school bus to a smaller town and then took off on foot, our backpacks leaning us forward so that we walked like hunchbacks, to a village at the edge of Lake Atitlán. I still talk to myself about Guatemala. Eighteen years and I write it out on restaurant tables with my finger. I once read that Debussy used to play songs on the closed piano lid. Sometimes he didn't want to actually hear the music?

We took a room in a one-room inn run by a stooped, crippled Pole. He spoke with a British accent he said he picked up during the war. He told us he flew for the RAF until the Nazis shot him down over France. Military pension. Washed up in Guatemala in the early '60s and never left. He discoursed in that sing-song English about homemade wine and death squads. He said once in a while the natives need to be reminded that they're natives. "Though I must emphasize that, of course—" One tap of his cane. Another tap of his cane. "—that on a personal level I quite detest killing."

In the afternoons a little girl brought us coffee to a table on the edge of the shore. She was lanky, eyes big as full moons. She curtseyed, while still balancing the tray atop one palm. Eyed us, separately, for a moment before setting down the coffees and backing away. When the tide came in, it washed over the legs of the table.

"Think she's his?" she said.

"Whose?"

"The codger."

"You think he can still get it up?"

"Isn't that myth? Never met a single one who couldn't."

Our room looked out upon the lake and in the morning, out of the mist, the cone of the volcano rose up out of the water.

At night, it rained. I'd go out and stand on the beach in the still sun-heated rain.


Toward dawn, on our last night, I woke up and she was sitting on the edge of the bed, wearing only a T-shirt and her headband.

"You can't sleep?"

"It doesn't matter."

"Is it Mike?"

"Who's Mike?"

"The guy, you know, from Spanish immersion."

"Chris."

"So, Chris?"

"What about him?"

"What happened to your arm?"

"You think Mike beat me up?"

"Chris—"

"I tripped on a hole running in Antigua. Good health care. I didn't pay a thing."

She leaned back and spoke to the ceiling fan whose blades rotated slowly above us like we were in an Antonioni movie. She spoke, if I remember, for a long time to the ceiling fan. Life and death and sweat—we couldn't take off enough those nights—and I can't remember a single thing she said. About me she once said that I could never see the forest for the trees. It's a phrase I still don't understand. Aren't the trees the forest? I remember the day we met and I rode home no-handed through the Presidio Cemetery and sang to the graves. Insane to be that happy, get you arrested by the park police—

We used to play a game where we'd pretend we'd just met.

"I'm Harv. Sorry, I didn't catch your—"

"Diane Somerville. Human Resources."

"Terrific to meet you, Diane. What brings you to the office party, the office party?"

"Look, I got to go feed my cats."

She's in Seattle now. A political scientist, which to me is a hilarious job title. Sometimes I call her.

"Hello?"

I pant a little into the phone.

"Harv? Harv Nadelson?"

"In the flesh."

"You're naked?"

"Sure."

"Gross. Fat now?"

"Getting there."

"Nice, fat guys are in. Chubby dads—"

"What happened with that guy?"

"Which one?"

"Spanish immersion."

"Oh, Atitlán, the volcano. You were a hero, Harv. You saved me. Is that what you want to hear?"

"Yes."

"How are you?"

"I don't know."

The old Pole said he wouldn't go back to Europe in a box. ❧

*Peter Orner is the author of several books, most recently the story collection* Maggie Brown & Others *(Little, Brown), and holds the Dartmouth Professorship of English and Creative Writing at Dartmouth College. His stories "Naked Man Hides" and "Pacific" appeared in Issue No. 115.*

# BEFORE AND AFTER

ELIZABETH REICHERT

When I was a child, I lived, for rather a short period, on the outskirts of a military base in Ohio, a place called Lockbourne, not in the subsidized base housing, as the other military families did, but outside of the gates, because my mother wanted us to have a normal life, which meant, for her, time spent with families who didn't worship their hero husbands.

My father was a hero, an American. My mother, British. They met on the coast of Malta, during World War II, when my father was flying as a hired hand for the Royal Air Force. My brother and I were born at this base, but I don't seem to have any recollections of the place to recreate a real picture. What I remember most is leaving, flying to what my father assured me was our other home. We took the British Overseas Airways Corporation, just British Airways now, flew a DC-6 prop aircraft, though my father wanted to fly the Comet. I know about such planes from him but it was my brother who took an interest. Father paraded us around the bases, quizzing us about where the gunners lay in the B-47s. Where were the Tornadoes and the Superfortresses? I'd get smacked for giving a wrong answer. Now I wonder what my father would have made of me taking these enormous 747s nonstop from North America to Asia, making more money than he could have dreamed of, and figure he would have still preferred me in a military uniform.

My name is Jeffrey Dawkins and I think of myself as British, despite my American father. (Dawkins is, in fact, my mother's name.) This isn't an exact identity, as I've lived most my life in other territories. My wife tells me there are names for people like us. Trans-nationals is one. Expatriates, another. Third-culture children, lost souls—the last one, the fear-mongering title of the identity theory book that she began writing when we were considering having children. I have always thought of us as citizens of the world, but my wife was worried about raising humans with a British American man brought up on the airfields of Malta and the States and an African-born French mother living in an old colonial outpost of the Far East. We decided against those children in the end.

My wife's name is Elodie, and I met her in what seems like another lifetime. She grew up in Nigeria, her parents, French Christian missionaries. It was the first thing that brought us together, the fact that we had split identities. The second was her interest in a story from my past. Start at the beginning, she would say. She was studying to become a psychologist.

We got off that prop plane, I told her, and a convoy of representatives was waiting for my father. He was a three-star brigadier general by then, and though convoy might not be the right word, I do remember several uniformed men and one black sedan that took us to the base. And yet, like I said, we didn't end up in one of the grand Tudors reserved on base for generals like my father, but in a ranch house, per my mother's more humble wishes—a ranch with a big American back deck that gave onto a great fenced-in sump pool.

When I first told my wife this story she had no equivalent in French to understand what a sump pool was. I explained it was just a field meant to collect runoff water from street gutters. With that water came trash, old bikes, a shopping cart someone had thrown in. My mother used to say that there were dead animals in there. My father would say, Look at

196   the goddamn sign. Trespassers would be thrown in jail by the State of Ohio. And did we think we'd become fighter pilots if we were thrown in jail by the State of Ohio?

Every house in our subdivision gave onto this thing, and in summer, blocked by trees, it could look like a velvety bog, and in winter, like a frosted pond. The only way to get inside, past the man-high fence, was to crawl through a hole in the foundation. I don't remember being afraid crawling inside.

Surely you were afraid, my wife would say. Just start over again.

I wasn't afraid. My father always said my mother had to abide the customs, learn the new rules in America, but in private, she'd tell us she hardly knew what the point could be. In her thick accent, always practicing her American—a *trunk* and not a *boot*; an *undershirt* and not a *vest*—and in dresses that never seemed as confident as the American women's, she would send us out in all manner of weather because surely we'd find a boy or two to play with.

But all the other children were inside that day, and there was nothing for us to do but wander the winter streets whipping each other with our scarves and pantomiming the insults of my hard-nosed father. "Abide the goddamn customs!" my brother shouted, puffing up his chest. "Read the goddamn sign!" But then he just gestured to the hole and we both ducked in.

On the other side of the fence, the sump had this clear edge you could walk around. My brother was shooting stones across the ice, I remember, or maybe a pinecone, as if testing it. I think the idea must have been that he would walk out onto the ice and retrieve some of the wheels poking through. If those wheels turned out to be bikes, then we'd have something better to do.

I'm certain I was told to stay put. As in, my brother was the only one who would know how to get the bikes out, so you be a good boy now, and you stay put.                                              **197**

So I stayed. And the ice on the sump held fine as my brother walked across. It was when he tugged up on one of the wheels that I remember the ice beginning to crack, and suddenly, my brother falling in. He was oddly bent over, too. Not straight. But curved to the water's surface, which must have only risen four feet or so. Maybe I couldn't see him well. It is something I have considered.

A friend I once told this to suggested I stayed because that's what I'd been told to do. It would have complicated things to tell him that, in fact, I had walked out onto the ice as soon as my brother fell in. I unwound the scarf from my neck and threw it to him because I'd probably had a misapprehension that my brother was in deep enough that the scarf would be of help to pull him out. In my dreams, my brother is often saying "the scarf, the scarf," but I can't remember if he actually said "the scarf," yet I am certain, because I saw it, that he did reach for my scarf and tug it under the water where it disappeared. The pieces of ice are doing the strangest tango across the water's surface in my memory, and then there I am, walking backward, away from him.

Start at the beginning, my wife would say. Just start over again.

Okay, I did imagine the belt, I tell her, but I'm also aware that the fullness of this picture might be confused with the memory where my father actually uses his belt to beat my brother when he catches us pantomiming him. He slips the belt out, chases my brother though the house, grips his arm so hard his bone will be fractured. In my dreams that scarf often becomes my father's belt, and though my brother grabs it, I'm never able to pull him out. What I do next in the dreams is yell. But it was the neighbor who yelled. He was on the other side of the sump, far from us, and he kept yelling my father's name as he ran the length of the fence. I'm not even sure I heard this man's voice, the screaming I mean, because what I can still see is the man's open mouth, the black,

198  gaping cry for help, the violence coming *at* me, and afterward, the wide quiet, snow beginning to fall, the steps going soundless, a clean cold wind rustling the crooked limbs around that landscape where everything was suddenly lost.

By the time they got inside, my brother was dead. *Boy Drowns in Sump.* That's what the papers would say. My brother had been caught beneath metal debris that you couldn't see on the surface and he'd gone into hypothermic shock: my brother slowly losing his consciousness and taking in water he didn't have the energy to get out. I would learn later that it can take fifteen minutes or more for this shock to set in. And me, I was standing there the whole time, thinking what? That my brother was trying to get the bike out? That my father would beat us with his belt? Or worse, did I stand there doing nothing, relishing the trouble to be had?

As my friend pointed out, I stood there because my brother had demanded it. But surely there was more, wasn't there? A teacher I tearily confessed to said it was perfectly natural for a younger sibling to hate an older brother. A friend's mother told me my mother should have known better sending us boys out into such weather. And my wife's take was that I must have frozen because I was terrified of my difficult father. See how every time you begin with your father?

Now all of this seems like another lifetime as well. I was in a pub when I first told Elodie this story. I was twenty-four. She was twenty-three. She slid into the booth beside me and whispered, "It is not your fault." I'd never expected to be warmed again by such tenderness, and as I'm sure it is with any marriage, her sense of my emotional territories, her way of maneuvering through them, of shining a light on some parts, while darkening others, have shaped me into the man I've become.

She is a small woman, Elodie, thin and frail, with blond hair she pulls from her face and hands she moves with a fluttering speed only to alight them calmly and affectionately on me, pulling me down to a place where I can make sense of things. I knew from the start I'd marry her if she would have me. I've never wanted to be far from her. Even now, I still don't want to be far from her.

We moved abroad almost immediately after our wedding, having decided on a new place, not America and not Britain, not France and not Nigeria. When my bank had a posting to the Far East it seemed an easy choice to make. Over the years, that post became a budget analyst position, followed by a financial management job, and Elodie began her own psychotherapy firm, charging a premium to wealthy expat clients. Our careers were the focus of our life now, along with our home at the top of Victoria Peak. Elodie was protective of me. She never did bring up my past, not even when we were discussing the implications of having children, and I had a fear, naturally, that in becoming a father myself I would have to face my own again. In our worst moments, my history could surface abstractly, Elodie accusing me of drawing away because I felt guilty, fearing I'd hurt those I loved. But after her anger passed, she would always come back to me.

It became a ritual for us. Start at the beginning, she would say. And with her, and within this comfortable life that we worked so hard to build in Hong Kong, I came to a point where I stopped thinking my brother's death had defined me.

Then, in my early fifties, and at the height of my banking career, a good decade before the Handover in Hong Kong, I began volunteering at a prison on the south side of the island and I came to another point when I would never be able to think such a thought again.

My wife and I decided to give back. There wasn't much more to it than that. She was the one who brought home the pamphlet for the program, calling the place a correctional facility and not the prison that it was. The Prisoners' Friends Association involved a rigorous,

**200** paper-logged interview, but once that was complete I was set up to visit with an inmate for an hour each week.

I drove early Saturday down past Stanley to this old colonial building forced up against Tai Tam Bay. I had to deposit everything from my pockets, pens and pencils that could be used as weapons. I was to wear a name tag and sit in a windowless room at a card table with my hands on the table's surface so they could be seen at all times. The program did not assign us any Class A prisoners. No murderers. But I did develop a picture of my inmate. I saw him as a Chinese kid, dragon tattoos up his arms, a foolish gambler who'd lost everything in Macau, some sort who had been pulled into the dominant crimes we had in Hong Kong back then—gangs and money laundering.

Only when the guards brought him in did I see that my prisoner was an older man, a sag in his face, the skin at his cheeks hanging down ever so slightly. Swaying his head back and forth, he held out his bony hand. He was an Indian man.

"My name is Harij Basak," he said. "But please, sir, call me Hari."

Hari is a different spelling, of course, but it was my brother's name, Harry.

"We can't assign you another inmate, no," the social worker told me. "Mr. Basak is our only English-speaking inmate." Two decades in Hong Kong and I still didn't speak much Cantonese. "Surely he hasn't harmed you, has he?" Harm? Of course not, I said.

The next week Hari sat forward. "They tell me you do not want me?" he said.

I had told the story so many times about my brother I didn't see any problem telling this man, especially if it meant he would see I had nothing against him.

"Wait," Hari said, interrupting me. I'd come to the point where I was standing by the sump. "I understand," he said. "For me it is my son who is gone. And the fact that I didn't save him? *That* is my prison—not this place."



"What is it?" my wife said when I got home that night. I didn't answer her, and she handed me a glass of wine. "Jeffrey," she said, "start at the beginning."

Maybe it was his name I told her. Or the moment he said, "You don't want me." Or maybe it was this prison he drew up in my mind. "I don't think it's comparable," I said. "A dead son and my brother's accident?"

Elodie told me I was right. It was foolish to conflate this Hari with my Harry, or myself with him. Then again, confrontation with a shadow self was only a natural defense when processing trauma.

"How long has it been since you thought of your brother? It's a coincidence is all."

Any associations I continued to make between my life and Hari's I decided to keep as my own.

I began to see Hari every week, in this last year or so before his release. I learned a lot about his son in the beginning. How he had been nineteen when he had left his family in Hyderabad to find higher paying work in Hong Kong. He had fallen in with the wrong people. Triads, Hari said. Gangs. He had started transporting drugs, not knowing how much trouble he'd be in when he lost a shipment. By the time Hari had come to help, the lost money had been on his son's head for six weeks. "What was a father to do? We do not have this kind of money." So Hari tried to burglarize a jewelry store, hoping his wife could sell the diamonds back home. He was on trial when he found out from his lawyer that his son had been murdered. Hari was given fifty-eight months in prison, though he hadn't stolen a single jewel.

"Three minutes standing there wondering where the safe could be, and every second, my son's life in my hands. I ask you again, what was a father to do?"

I posed the same question to Elodie that night and she seemed to consider it. "He wasn't thinking right," she said. "Hopefully he isn't aware of that."

We were sitting on our balcony, the city rising below, glowing in its rubies, emeralds, blues. I'd always been given the impression that, having climbed the rungs of society, we were protected from the hard facts of life down below. Hong Kong was so qualitatively different from anywhere I'd lived, from my parents' lives: the typhoon scares and incomprehensible Chinese all around us, the hellscape heat, the lush smog, all of it disguised that suburban winter of my childhood where my life had taken such a grave turn.

Our balcony was my wife's favorite spot, too, though she found it not so much a space of security as one of wonder—wonder, for one thing, at the fact we had been here long enough to watch the buildings climb up all around us.

This is how she would talk whenever an uncomfortable light began to shade our marriage: How much time had passed? Might we be stuck? Often she would take two glasses of wine onto the balcony and wait for me when we were falling on the old used-up arguments of our marriage—that I was turning away from her because I feared hurting her; that my distance was unkind; that she'd prefer that I work less.

That night, I knew it was time to draw closer to her again. But when I rose to put my hand on her shoulder, the distance to everything else seemed too great to bridge.

"Please, Jeffrey," she said, grabbing my hand. "Just stay. Tell me about that man."

So I told her about Hari's son.

I began to tell Elodie everything, thinking the more fully I was able to shape Hari in my wife's mind, the more exceptional he seemed, and the more exceptionally bad his circumstances. He'd had a love marriage. A Muslim woman named Noor. Her family had a diamond and pearl business that he would never work for. Instead, he'd cooked in restaurants, first as a fry chef, then as a head chef. Later, he got an MBA, because, as he'd said, he would not be a slave to another man's restaurant. He would open his own, show his father-in-law.

He liked to discuss ideas: "What else do you have when they take away your freedom but your ideas?" On history: "The princely states fared much better than those under the British Raj." On the future of Hong Kong: "Of course they'll take back the city, this is what happens after colonial rule." He spoke Hindi, Urdu, Telugu, English, and in prison had picked up Tagalog and Cantonese. I saw him as a man wronged.

"But he made a terrible decision," Elodie insisted. "How much money might it have taken for him to disappear with his son?"

I wanted to tell her I understood. I wanted to tell her that if we'd had children, we might have done the same.

And yet, at the same time, I worried she would think my sympathies misaligned. So there were things I did not tell Elodie—how talk about Hari's difficult father-in-law often led to talk about my father. I had told Hari about growing up on military bases, about the beatings with the belt. When I painted a picture of my father, cigarette in his mouth, damning all the people that men of his generation typically damned— Germans and Koreans to start with, defectors and Democrats—Hari mimicked his father-in-law, who also hated anyone who wasn't precisely like himself. He was great at impersonations, and though Hari brought face to this elderly man who hoarded his jewelry business while wagging a finger at his son-in-law who would never be good enough for his bright light—a man, in other words, very different from my father—I couldn't help but see my brother puffing up his chest and saying *Abide the goddamn customs. Read the goddamn sign.*

Nor did I tell Elodie that sometimes, after my visits with Hari, I would have these fantasies about what my brother would be like today. And every time this happened I knew Elodie was right, I shouldn't entertain such comparisons. But that didn't make the echoes, even those of my own devising, any less haunting.

Maybe I wanted to stay in a place where Elodie hadn't erased the complications of my past. But, then, I don't know. I'm not the psychologist in the family.

Hari's release date drew close and he became fixated on what he would do with the rest of his life. The social workers had told us to encourage such conversations so that, through our relationship, he would be given the confidence to again face society. I assumed Hari would return to Hyderabad, but he told me his wife felt he wouldn't be able to return. "I've brought shame upon our family," he explained, "what I've let happen to my son." Having been accredited in prison through the Construction Industry Council Training Academy, Hari was thinking he could find a job in road repairs. I asked around at work, ended up having lunch with an Indian colleague who I knew belonged to the Indian Recreation Club. This man offered to introduce me to a fellow on the board for my friend. I hadn't planned on escorting Hari to the club, but when I found out he had plans to take the bus to a halfway house, I decided I could provide a ride at least and make the introduction.

Walking out of the prison that day, Hari stopped, as if unsure how to approach me. He was wearing a faded pair of American blue jeans covered by a silk purple kurta. I walked around the car to greet him. "A new start?" I said, and he threw his arms around me, pounded on my back as if we were two lost mates from uni.

We drove toward the harbor, around the west side of the island, descending into the city. Hari couldn't believe how green the mountains were, how sudden the water.

"You could smell the sea in prison," he said. "And now, there she is."

The man at the Indian Club hired Hari on the spot, saying they could use a fill-in cook. The man also had an uncle in real estate. We went to look at a small flat, and because Hari was to work for the landlord's nephew, he was not only advanced the money for a deposit but trusted to supply the paperwork once the club secured his visa.

I must be behind his luck, Hari believed, and so he insisted I allow him to cook for me. We wandered a market, Hari haggling in his surprising Cantonese—lamb, cabbage, spices, a knife, oil, bowls. His flat was one room, with the typical Hong Kong windows, gated and small. There was only one burner and a fridge the size of which I hadn't seen since my student days. Nevertheless, Hari expertly prepared for us biryani and mutton cabbage rolls, homemade chapatti and mango chutney.

"This was the last meal that I had with my wife," he told me. "Not just any biryani but Hyderabadi biryani. You know how often I thought of this meal?"

Hari was making plans to save money, to see his wife. When I left him that evening, stumbling out into the empty streets of Kowloon, I turned over my shoulder, a little tipsy, and waved goodbye. I wasn't sure I'd see him again.

Spring came, and with it, the Hong Kong rains, the foggy steam rising up from the harbor to hang hazy around our home on the peak. I was back to weekly trips for the bank. Elodie was busy with her clients. So when Hari showed up at our door I barely recognized him. He'd contacted that Indian colleague, a man he saw often at the Indian Recreation Club. That man had given him my address. Hari must have gained forty pounds at least, his belly now pressing against that same purple

206 kurta, his hair feathered back in the way of the '80s. When he hugged me, I realized he was in fact a large man and not that bag of bones I'd come to know sitting across from him in the prison. He pulled away and a woman came forward, her hair in a bun, her eyes lined in kohl.

"This is my wife," Hari said proudly. "Noor."

I could smell the scent of sandalwood.

Noor handed my wife a folded sari and bowed before her in gratitude. I stepped back, surrounded by the buzz of an anxiety I couldn't place. Everyone was confessing they'd heard so much about the other, but I was worrying Hari might act subserviently. The only moment that approached any obsequiousness, though, was when Noor insisted on taking my hands and calling me "kind Sir." She held my eyes and tilted her head sideways, not as if inspecting me, but rather as if trying to communicate some deeper understanding.

"I wanted to thank you, kind Sir, for seeing my husband as a man and not as a criminal."

I suppose I could say this memory causes me a sorrow I never knew I could feel.

When Hari and Noor left, my wife sat at our table, clasping her hands. Her blond hair had gone silver, the deepening bow of her spine tender to me. I sensed in her an excitement particular to older and childless women who latch on to change in the lives of younger people when there isn't much change in their own.

"I could help them," she was saying. "But only if you think it is right."

When Elodie said "right," I knew she meant *safe*. But nearly five years in prison for a failed burglary meant to save a child into drugs seemed a harsh sentence to me. I would have friends, later, who would not understand when I said I'd met Mr. Basak in prison and I learned quickly not to mention the connection. But I did, in this moment, hesitate, which seems my own lapse in judgment. I worried not about Hari's past but about class differences. When he and Noor had come into the house, I'd been aware of his one-room flat with the fridge the size of an icebox. That was the anxiety. When he'd walked out onto our balcony I had cringed, waiting for him to take in our rather spectacular view of the floating city. But Hari didn't even look at the horizon. He'd knelt beside the herbs my wife tended there, pinching the basil between his thumb and forefinger. Noor didn't look out either, too busy examining my wife's bracelet. Even now this seems a heartbreaking bit of evidence that they were genuinely interested in *us* because how many peers can I see by comparison entering our flat only to marvel over the harbor view from a place of awe or, more likely, covetousness?

When I told Elodie I was embarrassed throwing our wealth at them, that there might be something not right in that, she said, "How very British of you."

Elodie loved inviting our Chinese helper for dinner or the Filipina maids she used to tutor in English on the weekends. She also loved entertaining scrappy European Sinophiles who'd come East dreaming of adventure only to end up as primary school teachers. Her parents, themselves poor, had administered to even poorer Nigerians, and Elodie had never been ashamed of our money because, unlike myself, she had never been especially motivated by it; she had never felt the need to stand on her own.

This wasn't Britain, she told me. The whole point of being what I liked to call a citizen of the world was to live a boundaryless life alongside others.

"If we can help them, Jeffrey, we should. It's only right, don't you think? Maybe I could help her sell her jewelry."

I nodded. "What harm," I said, "could come from making a few phone calls?"

Now all of this seems like another lifetime as well. I'm in my late seventies and know better than any younger man how you can spend an entire existence parsing through the patterns, trying to work out when things came together and when they fell apart. Was it the phone calls or the pamphlet? The moment with the social worker? When could I have turned back?

Elodie made those calls, and what followed were some of the happier years of my life. Lunches were arranged and Elodie planned a cocktail party during which Noor gave all of Elodie's women friends outrageous discounts on diamonds and pearls. Noor supplied the stones for refashioning engagement rings, the birth gems for children's birthdays. A year in, Hari began asking me about applying for small business loans. I helped him at our bank, and with the loan he took out a lease on a shop front in Wan Chai and called his restaurant by his son's name. Noor and Elodie decorated the place with brass fixtures and bright colors and the restaurant began to draw a well-heeled Indian expat clientele. When Hari came to our flat, he was a restaurateur in a Western suit, his wife, an insider in Hong Kong's back-door gem trade.

We fell into a lively social schedule as well. Every other Saturday the wives would have tea at the club or our place. Hari and I spent those same Saturdays playing cricket at the Indian Club, where he was now a member, or golf in Shek O, where our club was. We were both abysmal sportsmen who used the exercise to blow off steam from the week only to settle in for a few pints and some talk. Sometimes we'd skip sports and travel inland, taking the tourist tram from the peak and ending up at St. John's Cathedral on Garden Road. This was a place that brought to mind any church in London but with the colonial touches of wicker pew backs and fetid Bibles. I wasn't religious but I liked the cool emptiness of the church. Hari wasn't religious, either, but he'd found comfort, he said, in pretending. Maybe it was because this church was similar to the prison, so far removed from our lives, but we began to again broach those subjects we had not talked about since Hari's release. He told me about his son mostly, whom he missed dearly, and his family, whom he also missed. He began to refer to his life as "before" and "after" and he encouraged me to talk about my own before and after. Did I miss my parents? he wondered. And did my brother ever come to me in happier dreams than the one where I threw him the scarf?

I understood then, when our talks turned more serious like this, that it was important for Hari to draw similarities between our paths, to see us both as men who had triumphed over loss. And in his company I became that man, a man who had been marked by tragedy but had risen above. This was quite different from what my wife had made me, of course: a man who had not been marked by his brother's accident so much as by his father's critical denial of love.

When we would leave the cathedral, I would often find myself refashioning my early memories of arriving in Hong Kong, just a banker trying to get ahead, into images of a man more willfully leaving his painful past behind, coming upon the Central Bank buildings to mastermind an escape, visiting that first Chinese tailor and stepping into a new fate. I felt again the freshness of the humid air, the promise of becoming someone else. Swinging our golf clubs against the views of the South China Sea, or emerging from this airy church, I understood that what I shared with Hari was surely the sort of friendship that had been eluding me for years.

After our walks, Hari and I would often find ourselves together for so long we'd stay in Central and invite the wives in for dinner. I'm not sure how to say this, but the Basaks were very much in love, coming from the brink of disaster, as they had, and I often found that I desired Elodie more after our evenings with them. I would reach for her, again like that younger man I once was, and though it was Elodie

210 I wanted, I often felt like an elemental man caught in his love for an elemental woman. Elodie would roll over and say, "My gosh, Jeffrey, you're bringing back memories." Once she talked about that hotel in London, the open window, the rain coming in. "Do you remember what I said?" Of course I did. "I don't want it to end," she'd been saying. "I don't want it to end."

Now I take that same walk I used to take with Hari, but back then the tallest building used to be the Jardine House and now the buildings rise to a hundred floors, the sodium light illuminating the underside of the polluted clouds like an all-night open sign. Every time I sit against those wicker pews, every time I smell the moldering Bibles, I think of what can never change. How long ago it was that Hari showed up at our door. How painful to remember the look of fear on his face.

"I didn't know where else to go," he was saying. His shirt was ripped open and one shoe was missing. His right eye was swollen and he was bleeding from his head. That's why the shirt was ripped open. He was holding half of it to his head.

They wanted the rest of the money, he was saying, his son's old creditors, the money that Hari hadn't been able to get the first time. The Triads had been watching him, how well he'd been doing, how he attended parties on the Peak. It was serious. They were threatening Noor. They knew where they lived.

"I gave them all my money. But I'm still a million short. I told them I don't have it, but they don't believe me, you see."

I often go back in my memory to make sure Hari didn't actually ask me for the money. Or that he didn't say it was because of his association with me that they didn't believe him. I'm almost certain he didn't say these things, that they were only implied, but I can't remember. I do remember he said, "They will kill her. You understand? I cannot go to the police. There isn't time." But all I could hear was a pulsing animal desire to turn away. I thought of my wife saying, *What would it have cost for him and his son to simply disappear?*, and I told him to go as far away as possible, to buy two plane tickets, to disappear.

"Wait," I said, going back inside. I did not invite him in. I returned with a roll of paper towels. I handed him the paper towels. "To stop the bleeding," I said.

In my dreams the scarf now becomes a roll of paper towels melting in the water, and Hari, not my brother Harry, is the one bent over, trapped in the ice. Sometimes I see myself in the dreams standing on our balcony, not looking down onto the city but onto a wide, empty harbor that has taken the shape of a gigantic iced-over sump. In the dreams I'm accompanied by an expansive silence, a pause of the sort when snow begins to fall and all will be lost. I'm not thinking of how Hari should have watched out for this. How he made a bad decision, as Elodie would say. I'm thinking I'm relieved to know myself in this solitude as that boy who does nothing, who is alone, obstructed and safe.

In the morning I woke early and hurried downstairs. When Elodie emerged I asked her if she had heard me last night. There'd been a neighbor, I said, knocking at the wrong door.

Then, on a Saturday morning, our coffee, the newspaper. Elodie dropped her cup and the porcelain pieces scattered everywhere. "Oh my God, Jeffrey. Oh my God!"

The picture of Noor in the paper was older, from when we'd first met her. The death had been brutal. I can hardly bring myself to confess it involved an ax. For weeks there was a warrant out for the arrest of the disappeared husband. The Hong Kong police worked to no avail with the Indian police. I was questioned because of my association with the prison and the loan from my bank. I answered every question, confirmed Hari's son had transported drugs for Triads, explained our friendship, and provided names of those in Hyderabad he spoke of often. After the police left, I felt there might be a way to tell Elodie that Hari had come to me before Noor's murder, that I had lied to her. But I thought of how she touched me, of how she brought me, frankly, into a world of love, and I couldn't bear her coming to an understanding that had escaped her for all of our years together.

Elodie was calling Hari's land line over and again, convinced he had left to protect us. But the police had told us his apartment had been deserted, two plates of food on the table, a detail I still cannot withstand.

Over time "they" began to hold all of my wife's anger. This was a tempting argument for myself as well: that I had not been involved in Noor's death. I remembered what people had said to me after my brother died. *No one could have stopped him. You stayed because your brother demanded it.* Sentiments that were perhaps true, but also false.

I also heard Elodie. *How unfair to return for the money after so many years. How fortunate Hari avoided his own death.* Sentiments, again, that might appear true but were not.

Never once did Elodie regret bringing home the pamphlet for the Prisoner's Friends Association or making those calls. Nor did she consider the possibility that Hari's relationship with us might have been the very thing that brought his past back. She did not think how it must have felt for me to say Hari, let's do lunch. Hari, I understand you. Hari, how have you been?

My mother didn't get within twenty feet of the sump. It was my father who hurtled his body over the barbed-wire fence over the spot the neighbor had tossed his coat—my father who freed my brother's leg and carried him out. Even in this act of heroics, even in this moment of extreme focus, he had enough sense to turn over his shoulder and glare back at me with a look I'll never forget.

After that, they took my mother away. Sedated, surely, and in a hospital from which she never did emerge. When the night came and there were no longer any people in our house, no policemen and no neighbors, my father said, "Why were you standing there, huh? You tell me that." I didn't answer him and my father and I never spoke again.

I do remember the funeral. There was a woman—Katherine, the mother of the friend who took me away to her house. She was the one who said my mother should have known better than sending us boys out into such weather. She cupped my face in her cold hand and shook her head.

It would turn out that I would see a lot of Katherine in the next few months, but not enough to get a sense of her beyond the displeasure with my mother and the authoritative palm under my chin. They—Katherine and my father—decided to send me to boarding school in England. My father ended up marrying her, and when he was transferred to another base, my mother was returned, also to Britain, where her family put her in a new hospital. For a while, I received letters from my mother's family. Then those, too, stopped. And in my last year before university, a guidance counselor sat me down and explained that a check had been sent with a letter announcing my emancipation. This woman had to tell me, *You ought to move forward in your life without them.*

I went to a psychologist about this several years before I met Elodie. This psychologist told me to explore how the family might have come apart even if Harry's accident had never taken place. I told her about my mother's dresses that weren't as confident as the American women's. I told her about the customs my mother didn't seem to understand, how she hated everyone worshiping my father as a hero. This psychologist wanted to know if, before my brother had walked out onto that sump, was I bothered that my mother couldn't hold it together for my father? My parents had been destined to drift apart, this therapist believed, and in this way I became convinced that what had happened to our family had been my mother's fault and not my own.

Then I met Elodie and it became easier to blame my father. He was the villain of the story, the way he beat us, and bullied us. My mother got to be the sick one, but my father had made a cruel choice, a choice, as Elodie said, that would strap any child with abandonment issues, leaving one prone to paralyzing separation anxiety all his life.

This sounded like jargon to me. The truth was, I could admire my father his heroic ruthlessness. I imagined tragedy coming to my loved ones, to Elodie, and I felt certain that if there were someone to blame, then blame I would. I understood my father and mother couldn't look at me. I was a source of pain that had to be erased. Elodie used to say that taking on the blame was foolish. Death was never personal. If you believe death is your fault, then it also follows you might be able to fix it. But you cannot fix death.

Sounds reasonable, right? And you wonder why I lied to her about Hari? Why I need her to believe I am a good man?

After I met Hari, I knew Elodie had to believe I wasn't the villain of this story because the boy who does nothing, who stands there essentially alone— that couldn't be the man she loves. When I walked up to my brother and threw him that scarf, I knew, no matter how young I was, no matter my father's beatings or my brother's demands, that something was terribly wrong. And as I would do with Hari, I felt an animal desire to turn away. Was it revulsion? Or an innate disgust in the face of horror? Or maybe only a desire to protect myself? Elodie always said I turned away because I was afraid to hurt those I loved. I think I turned away because I was not thinking of those I love.

Selfishness.

You'd think a therapist or my wife or even Hari would have provided a simple word like that.

A couple of years ago I tried to look for Hari online. But what was I going to say to him when the costs of turning away had been so severe?

Don't we all look away? Don't we all have our excuses, especially us citizens of the world, who belong nowhere and to no one in the end?

Elodie found me at the computer. "What's wrong?" she said, touching my shoulder. When I didn't answer her, she said, "Start at the beginning."

But I'd lost the ability to share that ritual with her, lost it so many years before.

Now I take that same walk every Saturday and I sit in the cathedral alone. How many people pass through your life like this, when you are one of these so-called citizens of the world, touching you irrevocably before they go? The truth is, there have been others like the Basaks through the years, others who were far removed from our station in life, but no one who was a true friend, no one like Hari, and no tragedy as impossible as Noor's. In my dreams I now find myself asking Hari where is the before and the after? Where? Where did I go wrong? But he isn't listening, as he's stuck in that ice, or he is walking out of the ice, on top of the water—away. And I stand there, in that prison of the mind that only Hari can understand, calling myself by many awful names, feeling fallen and expelled. When I sit in the cathedral, I imagine going into one of those confession booths and telling the priest, Father, I have sinned. *Father.* And I would not tell him about my brother or the scarf, the paper towels or the ax. I would tell him about all the moments with my wife when I lie to her so we can keep believing I'm someone I am not. The sump would warm after my confession and the water would evaporate and for a minute that place in my dreams would become an empty field without the need for a hero. I would hold Harry's chin. And I would invite Hari in. And I would return to my wife and be able to answer her honestly when she says to start at the beginning. ❧



........................................................................................................

*Elizabeth Reichert lived in Hong Kong for eight years. Her work has appeared in* Tin House.

RAIN OR SHINE
ROCK THE WEEVIL ANYTIME
PRINTED ON PREMIUM APPAREL AND AVAILABLE IN A RANGE OF UNISEX SIZES
ZYZZYVA
LOGO TEES & HOODIES NOW AVAILABLE
WWW.ZYZZYVA.ORG/SHOP

# COMMUNITY SUPPORT
## FOR LITERATURE & THE ARTS

18 Reasons

Alexander Book Company

Bird & Beckett Books & Records

The Booksmith

City Lights Bookstore

Green Apple Books

Humboldt Distillery

Mechanics' Institute

Pegasus Books

Poets & Writers

Rare Bird Books

Rutgers University Press

Santa Monica Review

Stanford Continuing Studies

Skylight Books

Virgin Hotels

## ADDITIONAL SUPPORT PROVIDED BY

# ZYZZYVA

# A SAN FRANCISCO JOURNAL OF ARTS & LETTERS.

*ZYZZYVA publishes the best in prose, poetry, and visual art from emerging and renowned writers and artists.*

**$42** 4-ISSUE SUBSCRIPTION

**$70** 8-ISSUE SUBSCRIPTION

**$30** 4-ISSUE STUDENT SUBSCRIPTION

"One of the country's finest literary journals."

**—The Washington Post**

PLEASE SEND PAYMENT BY CHECK TO
**57 POST ST. SUITE 604, SAN FRANCISCO, CA 94104**
OR SUBSCRIBE ONLINE AT:

# WWW.ZYZZYVA.ORG

CITY LIGHTS
A COMMUNITY
center
for BOOKS
And
FREE
THINKERS

BIRD &
BECKETT
BOOKS AND RECORDS

GREEN APPLE
BOOKS & MUSIC

ALL KINDS
OF BOOKS
FOR
ALL
KINDS
OF PEOPLE
SKYLIGHT
Books

STAY
VIRGIN
HOTELS

STAY WILD. STAY PROUD. STAY REBELLIOUS.

This is your place in the city. Come grab a coffee at Funny Library Coffee Shop, dinner at Commons Club or a rooftop cocktail at Everdene.

Book Now: Chicago & San Francisco
Coming Soon: Dallas & Nashville

Virgin HOTELS
SAN FRANCISCO

VIRGINHOTELS.COM/SAN-FRANCISCO
@VirginHotelsSF

# Poets&Writers
## 50 & FORWARD

Since our founding in 1970, writers have turned to us for inspiration, guidance, and community.

Our vision is to empower creative writers and strengthen literary communities for decades to come.

**Visit pw.org**

*"I regularly send my students to Poets & Writers' website, an invaluable free resource, putting a wealth of information at their fingertips—information it would take one lone writer untold hours (or years?) of sleuthing to compile."*

TRACY K. SMITH